RECALL
TOTAL ENGLISH

RECALL
TOTAL ENGLISH

by

D. D. VUJIC

BELL HARBOUR PRESS
DUNEDIN, FLORIDA

Published by Bell Harbour Press, www.bellharbourpress.com
Printed in the United States of America

Library of Congress Control Number: 2025907054

To contact the author, visit his website at **https://ddvujic.com**m
Email: **d.dan.vujic@gmail.com**

DEDICATION

This book is dedicated with heartfelt gratitude to all my past and present students.

The development of the Recall Total English method and the creation of this book have been inspired by all of you—from CEOs in boardrooms across Japan to truck drivers navigating the roads of Egypt and everyone between.

This work represents not only years of research and development but also the over 15,000 hours spent teaching online, working with over 8,000 students from diverse backgrounds and cultures from around the world. Each lesson, each interaction, and each breakthrough moment has contributed to the methodology presented in these pages.

I am endlessly grateful to have been part of your learning journey. Your stories and successes have shaped this book and deepened my understanding of what it means to teach and learn. Thank you for letting me be your guide in developing your English language skills and for helping me continuously refine this unique method.

D. D. Vujic

INTRODUCTION

Welcome to a unique English learning experience! Whether you've been studying English for years or just beginning your journey, this book offers a refreshingly unique approach to language learning that differs from traditional methods.

This book combines years of scientific research on how we learn languages and how our brains function, along with my 24 years of experience teaching English as a second language (ESL). The methods in this book have been implemented in a real classroom since 2019 and have helped thousands of students worldwide, from shy beginners to more experienced learners.

WHO THIS BOOK IS FOR

This book is designed for readers with a minimum B1 level (B2 recommended) on the Common European Framework of Reference (CEFR) established by the Council of Europe. More simply, if you can watch English movies without your native subtitles and recognize familiar English phrases, this book will benefit you.

WHAT THIS BOOK IS NOT

This is not your average English course. You won't find yourself drowning in complex grammar rules or suffering through endless vocabulary memorization sessions. There are no boring studies that leave you questioning your progress.

This book focuses on action. It is for people who want to develop their existing English skills to a fluent level.

WHAT THIS BOOK DOES

This book serves as a guide to help you use the English you already know. You can achieve fluency by recalling from your subconscious mind the English you already know; this is done by using popular media—such as movies, TV series, audiobooks, video games, YouTube, and podcasts. Pedro, a computer engineer from Brazil, explained it well: "I had been collecting parts of English for years but keeping them in different boxes. Your method taught me to combine all those parts to make something helpful. Now, I don't feel like I'm just studying English. I'm using it in my life!"

FORMAT RECOMMENDATIONS

If you are now reading this book's digital or paperback version, pair it with the audiobook for maximum benefit. Hearing the book after or before reading the digital or paperback versions will significantly improve your understanding.

When you listen to things explained, it helps your brain understand them better than just reading. The audiobook also shows you how to pronounce words and how people usually speak. Sophia, a marketing executive from Italy, said she listens to audiobooks on her way to work and reads the digital version at night. "Hearing the same text explained twice, in different formats, really helped me better understand the story," she explained.

THE IDEA THAT WE NEED "MORE VOCABULARY" ISN'T TRUE

Here's an interesting fact: Native English adult speakers typically know around 20,000 to 30,000 unique words. Those with higher education may know between 30,000 and 40,000. In writing and conversation, whether at work or in personal life, native English adult speakers usually use only 3,000 to 5,000 unique words daily.

You might wonder what native English adult speakers do with the other 17,000 to 37,000 words they know. The answer is simple: nothing. Those words remain locked in their minds, waiting to be used someday or not.

Carl, a business analyst from Germany, laughed when he heard this. I've been working hard to memorize difficult words that even people who grew up speaking the language hardly use. That's both annoying and comforting!"

It's important to know that just knowing words is not the same as learning how to use them. You might recognize a word and understand its meaning but still struggle to use it correctly in conversation. This book will teach you how to effectively use the words you already know, focusing on the most commonly spoken 3,000 to 5,000 words—all you need for everyday English at work and home.

THE PRONUNCIATION PRIORITY

Pronunciation is even more important than vocabulary or grammar; it's key. What good is a fantastic vocabulary if your listeners can't understand you?

You can only learn proper pronunciation by listening. No book alone can teach you how to pronounce words correctly—you must hear them to understand them.

Yuki, a product manager from Japan, discovered this the hard way. "I had learned the word focus from reading, and I pronounced it as fah-kuss for months. No one corrected me until a kind colleague finally explained it should sound like foh-kus. I had been saying it wrong in every meeting!"

THE PERSONAL LEARNING PATH

Every brain is unique and learns differently. That's why the Recall Total English method, which focuses on recalling and using the English you already know, empowers YOU to choose your learning materials! You are in control of your learning journey.

- Do you enjoy video games? Use them!

- Do you like movies or TV shows more? Learn from them!

- Maybe you prefer news or audiobooks and podcasts? Perfect—use them instead!

By selecting materials that interest you, learning becomes fun and exciting, which has always been the most effective way to learn. Learning from materials you enjoy makes you more likely to stay engaged, which can lead to quicker and more effective learning.

Martina, an Italian fashion designer, was surprised by how much quicker she learned when she stopped pushing herself to study business English textbooks and began watching fashion documentaries and designer interviews instead. "For the first time, I wasn't counting the minutes until my English study time was over," she told me. "Instead, I was losing track of time because I was so engaged with the content."

A NOTE ABOUT MUSIC AND LANGUAGE LEARNING

In this book, we will look at different media types, but I want to point out that although music is popular, it has significant limitations as a tool for learning languages. Music lyrics often use poor grammar and unusual word structures, trading linguistic accuracy for rhythm, rhyme, and emotional impact. Songs often use incomplete sentences, old slang, and intentionally incorrect grammar.

Tariq, an IT engineer from Morocco, learned this lesson the hard way when he kept saying, "I ain't doing nothing" in professional settings because he'd heard it in popular songs. His American colleagues gently explained this was a double negative and not appropriate in business communication.

This doesn't mean you should avoid English language music entirely. Songs can help with rhythm, cultural references, and certain pronunciation parts. Be careful not to use lyrics as models for how to speak or write correctly in everyday situations.

A WORD ON LANGUAGE LEARNING DURING SLEEP

Later in this book, we will explore an interesting method many students find helpful: listening to English while sleeping. Your brain doesn't completely stop working during sleep; it stays active, processing information and strengthening memories. This ongoing brain activity allows for passive language learning, which I will explain later.

Many students report benefits from falling asleep while

listening to English audio at a low volume. Fatima, a small business owner from Morocco, described it this way: "After a few weeks of playing English podcasts while I slept, I noticed words coming to me more easily in conversation. Was I actually learning while asleep? I'm not sure, but something definitely improved!"

While we'll explore this approach's science and practical applications in later chapters, I mention it now because it highlights an important truth: language learning happens in ways that extend beyond conscious study or traditional means. Your brain continuously processes language, even when you're unaware of it.

THE READINESS CHECK

One final note before we begin: If you haven't fully understood what you've read so far, your current English level might not be compatible with this book. You may not receive the full intended benefit. Don't get frustrated—simply set the book aside, work on developing your English to a higher level, and then return when you feel more prepared.

How can you tell if you're ready? Ask yourself these questions:

- Could I explain the main idea of this introduction to someone else?

- Do I understand at least 70% of what I've read without translation?

If you answered "yes" to these questions, you're ready for the journey ahead!

WHAT TO EXPECT IN THE COMING CHAPTERS

In the pages that follow, we'll explore:

- How your brain stores and accesses language.

- Why traditional study methods often fail to produce fluency.

- How different media forms can activate different parts of your English.

- The important role of confidence in language performance.

- How to develop a personalized English practice plan.

- Techniques for managing your accent and improving pronunciation.

- Methods for thinking directly in English instead of translating in your head.

- How to use Artificial Intelligence (AI) to develop your English further.

- And much more!

Are you ready to discover the English in your brain, waiting to be activated? Let's begin the journey!

CHAPTER 1

THE WORLD'S GREATEST STORAGE SYSTEM IS THE HUMAN BRAIN

Have you ever had this surprising experience? You're watching a movie or listening to someone speak English, and suddenly, you understand a word or phrase you don't remember learning. Where did that understanding come from? The answer might surprise you: your brain has been quietly collecting English all along, storing away bits and pieces even when you weren't studying.

Think of your brain as having two main storage areas: a big warehouse (your long-term memory, managed by the hippocampus) and a small room (your active memory, managed by the cerebral cortex).

The warehouse can hold nearly infinite information, while the small room has limited space for the words you use every day. I like to explain it to my students using the "warehouse " vs. small room" metaphor.

To actually use information stored in your long-term memory, your brain must transfer it to active memory through a process called consolidation. Think of consolidation as putting information on standby, making it ready for instant use; much like your computer is on standby while powered on but not in use, so is the hippocampus. Imagine your long-term memory as an enormous warehouse containing every book you've ever read, everything you ever heard and seen, felt, and smelt, while your active memory is like a small room that can only hold a limited amount of information at a time. When you need information not in the small room, your brain sends a request to the "warehouse" to transfer what it needs to the room. This typically takes a few seconds, but sometimes, it takes much longer to retrieve the information; this is why sometimes you know that you know something but can't quite recall it immediately—the warehouse is being searched, but what you need is not found right away, this occasionally happens because the warehouse is so big and there is so much information packed in it.

Consolidation doesn't always work perfectly on the first try. Factors like your age, how old the memory is, and its importance to you can affect this process. When consolidation first fails, your brain keeps trying until it succeeds—which explains why you sometimes can't remember something right away but recall it an hour later. This happens to everyone, even native English speakers, with their own language!

Elena, a software developer from Ukraine, experienced this: During an important job interview, she couldn't remember the word "deadline" despite knowing she knew it.

Two hours later, the word suddenly popped into her mind while riding the bus home.

"It was like my brain kept searching even when I had moved on to other things," she explained. "So frustrating that it couldn't find it when I actually needed it!" This delayed recall is actually your brain working as designed—it doesn't give up just because you've consciously moved on to something else, it will search until it finds it. What's impressive about your brain is that no memory truly disappears under normal circumstances unless the brain experiences a disease like Alzheimer's, which can significantly affect memory retrieval; other factors include suffering a stroke or enduring an injury from an accident. The hippocampus has a nearly limitless storage capacity if unfortunate illness or injury does not occur. It can continue to record and store memories throughout your entire life.

Scientists have discovered that people under hypnosis or during certain types of brain stimulation can recall information they had no idea they had—detailed memories from early childhood, passages from books read decades ago, or conversations they didn't realize they had paid attention to. The information was there all along although they couldn't access it consciously.

"The brain is not like a computer hard drive that fills up," I tell my students. "It's more like a universe that keeps expanding to accommodate new stars."

YOUR HIDDEN ENGLISH VOCABULARY

Now, consider how many hours you've spent watching English language movies and TV shows, playing games, and reading books, articles, newspapers, and magazines. All those English words you've heard and read are recorded and stored in your long-term memory (hippocampus). You might have as many as 5,000 English words hidden in your long-term memory, yet you may be unsure how to use them correctly or even realize they exist there. The Recall Total English method will help you move these words to your active memory (cerebral cortex) and teach you how to use them actively instead of having them stored away in a passive state.

Let me share a story about my student, Bruno, an electrical engineer from Argentina. He had studied English formally for only one year but had been watching Hollywood movies with subtitles since childhood.

During one of our first classes, I used the word "endeavor," a reasonably advanced vocabulary word. To my surprise, Bruno immediately understood it.

"How do you know that word?" I asked. "We haven't used it in class."

Bruno thought for a moment, then smiled. "I think it was in a space movie...astronauts were saying it." He had unknowingly absorbed this word from a movie he'd watched years earlier. This is precisely why watching English movies is so powerful—you're constantly feeding your brain new words, phrases, and expressions that get filed away in your long-term memory, even when you're not consciously studying.

THE RECALL METHOD: WHY IT WORKS BETTER THAN RELEARNING

So, you need not learn thousands of more words because you likely know enough already. Remember, we use between 3,000 and 5,000 unique words daily. Once you learn how to use them, most of these words will be in your working memory as they are used daily, but then you have thousands of more words in your long-term memory if you need them.

Why relearn what you already know? Instead, this book will teach you how to move your existing knowledge from your long-term memory to your working memory while teaching you how to use these words effectively.

Some readers will see results faster than others. I'll explain why later, but you will improve your overall English much quicker than you may think.

Keiko, a game designer from Japan, described her experience with the recall method this way: "Before, I was always memorizing new words from lists. It was so much work, and I would forget them quickly. With the recall method, I feel like I'm not learning new English—I'm rediscovering English I already knew but couldn't use. It's like finding money in a coat pocket you forgot about!"

THE ILLUSION OF NOT KNOWING

One of the most common challenges for language learners is what I call "the illusion of not knowing." Many believe they don't have enough vocabulary when, in fact, they have a wealth of words—they struggle to recall them quickly or confidently.

Consider this common experience: You're watching an English movie with subtitles in your language. You read a subtitle and think, "Oh, that's what that means!" rather than "I've never heard that word before." That moment of recognition reveals that the English word was already in your brain somewhere; you couldn't retrieve it until you saw the translation. Arjun, a computer engineer from India, tracked these "Oh, that's what that means!" moments while watching an episode of a TV show. In just 30 minutes, he experienced this recognition over 20 times. "I realized I already knew much more English than I thought," he said. "I just needed help remembering it."

ACTIVE RECALL VS. PASSIVE RECOGNITION

There's a big difference between recognizing words when you hear them (passive knowledge) and being able to use them in your speech (active learning). Most language learners have a much larger passive vocabulary than active vocabulary.

The difference can be huge—you will recognize 5,000 or more English words when you hear them but can only use 1,000-1,500 when speaking actively. The good news is that converting passive knowledge into active knowledge is much easier than learning new words.

Ahmed, a truck driver from Egypt, illustrated this perfectly. During a reading exercise, he understood a text having about 3,500 different English words. Yet when I asked him to tell me the story, he used fewer than 800 unique words. His passive vocabulary was over four times larger than his active vocabulary! After three months of practicing the recall methods, he was actively using 2,000 unique words, more than doubling his expressive capacity without learning many new words.

THE SLEEPING BRAIN: LEARNING WHILE YOU REST

How does this work? During sleep, your brain reviews and strengthens neural pathways formed during the day. When you provide gentle English input during this time, you give your brain additional material to process and consolidate. You're helping your brain's "night shift" organize your English knowledge more effectively.

The brain processes sound during sleep uniquely. Research suggests that the brain can still pick up the auditory rhythm and melody of language, even when we're unaware of them. This is because the brain's auditory cortex, responsible for processing sound, remains active during sleep. Through passive listening, the brain can continue to learn and absorb new information, including language patterns and vocabulary.

One of the best benefits of developing language skills while asleep is the potential for improved language recall. By exposing your brain to English input during sleep, you can strengthen new vocabulary and grammar rules, making it easier to remember them. This is especially useful for language learners who struggle to remember new words.

Research has shown that the brain can even reorganize and rewire itself during sleep, a process known as synaptic plasticity. This means that the connections between neurons in the brain can be strengthened based on the input received during sleep. Giving your brain gentle English input allows you to rewire your brain to understand and process English better.

Research has also shown that the brain can learn and consolidate new information on various topics, from math and science to music and art. However, language skills are particularly well-suited to sleep-based learning. A good sleep environment is essential to get the most out of sleep-based language learning. This means keeping the volume low, using a comfortable and supportive pillow, and avoiding distractions like bright lights or loud noises. Also, choose a podcaster audiobook that is engaging and easy to follow, with a clear and gentle narrator's voice.

The sleeping brain is a powerful tool for learning and consolidation, so why not try it? Put on your favorite podcast or audiobook, drift off to sleep, and let your brain do the rest.

NUMBER OF WORDS YOU KNOW
EQUALS YOUR UNDERSTANDING

Here's an encouraging fact: By knowing 1,000 of the most common English spoken words, you can understand about 35% of everyday conversations. Knowing 2,000 words increases that to 70%; with 3,000 words, you'll understand almost everything besides academic discussions. This means you don't need a bigger vocabulary to communicate effectively. Knowing 3,000 to 5,000 words is enough for everyday use at work and home. The average B1-level English student knows between 1,200 and 1,500 words. This means that the B1-level student only needs to learn another 1,500 to 1,800 more words to understand most of everyday English conversations, and the B2-level student needs to learn even fewer words. But that does not mean learning just any words.

LEARN THE RIGHT WORDS

Instead of trying to memorize an overwhelming number of words or phrases, focus on understanding and mastering the right words that are commonly used by native English speakers in everyday conversations. Pay attention to how these words are pronounced and the context in which they are used. Remember, it's not about how many words you know; what is essential is what words you know and how well you can use them.

You might be wondering what these 3,000 to 5,000 commonly spoken words are; for the answer, go to Google and start two searches: "What are the 3,000 most commonly spoken words in English". Google will produce hundreds of results, pointing you to websites that have published these words. When you review these sites, you will notice that nearly all have the same list of words. Repeat the search, but this time replace the number 3,000 with 5,000 and then compare the lists on various sites. You will note that, again, almost everyone has the same list. Copy and paste this list into a document, then make it your mission to learn these words, not just memorize them, but really know them.

BEYOND WORDS: THE CHUNKS OF NATURAL SPEECH

Another essential part of language stored in your long-term memory is what linguists call "chunks" or "formulaic sequences"—common phrases and expressions that native speakers use every day. Expressions like — "as far as I know," "to be honest," "you know what I mean," and "the thing is" function almost as single vocabulary items in natural speech. You've likely absorbed these phrases through countless exposures in movies, TV shows, and other English media.

Jessica, a software programmer from Brazil, experienced a breakthrough when she started focusing on these chunks instead of individual words. "I realized I didn't need to build sentences word by word like I was taught in school," she explained. "Many of these expressions were already in my head from watching American shows. When I used these chunks, my speaking became much more natural sounding."

THE EMOTIONAL MEMORY CONNECTION

Have you noticed how words and phrases tied to emotional experiences stick better in your memory? There's a scientific reason: your brain focuses on information with emotional importance. This explains why many students easily remember song lyrics, movie quotes, jokes, or even swear words in

English—they all carry emotional weight. We can use this natural tendency by linking English learning to positive emotional experiences.

Frank, a customer service specialist for a major car manufacturer in Germany, made impressive progress after joining an online gaming community where English was the common language. "I learned more useful English in three months of playing games with people from around the world than in three years of formal classes," he laughed. The language sticks better when you're having fun and making friends.

PRACTICAL EXERCISE: MINING YOUR MEMORY

Let's end this chapter with a practical exercise to start accessing the English already stored in your brain:

Media Inventory: List all the English language movies, TV shows, games, books, or websites you've engaged with over the years, even if you used subtitles or translations.

1.   **Phrase Collection**: For each item on your list, recall specific words, phrases, or expressions you remember from that source. Don't worry about spelling—note what comes to mind.

2.   **Recognition Test**: Find a short clip from an English movie or show you've never seen before. Watch it first without subtitles and note how much you understand. Then, watch again with subtitles in your language and count how many words you recognize once you see the translation.

3.   **Daily Activation**: Choose one source of English you enjoy and spend 15 minutes with it daily, actively noticing words and phrases you understand without translation.

Daniel, a tour guide from France, completed this exercise and was astonished to list nearly 100 English language movies he had watched and over 40 video games he had played. "I realized I had exposed myself to over a thousand hours of English without ever thinking about it," he said. "No wonder certain phrases and expressions felt familiar to me – I had heard them many times before!"

CHAPTER 2

USE IT OR LOSE IT

You've heard the idiom saying, "Use it or lose it," which applies perfectly to languages. While you won't forget the English you've learned, lack of practice makes accessing that knowledge increasingly difficult. Your brain constantly optimizes for efficiency.

It carefully moves rarely used information to long-term storage, freeing up valuable space in your active memory for information you access every day.

This means those English words, grammar rules, and conversational phrases you haven't used lately haven't disappeared—they're just harder to recall because your brain has filed them away in your long-term memory.

Prevent this by using your English skills regularly. With consistent practice, you'll quickly regain access to that knowledge and stop your brain from moving it deeper into long-term memory. The more you use a memory, the faster you can recall it. Regular practice lets you keep your English knowledge for immediate use with no delay.

People often ask me how long it will take to become more fluent using the Recall Total English method. This isn't a simple question to answer. Have you noticed that some people seem to learn languages faster than others?

There are several reasons for this: everyone's brain is unique, like a fingerprint.

Age is a significant factor determining why some people learn languages more quickly and easily than others. Research shows that the best age range for language learning is between 5 and 35 years old. Every year after 35, learning takes longer and becomes more difficult. Also, if your native language is similar to English, like "German", you have a significant advantage. Learning habits, consistent practice, and effective study strategies dramatically affect how quickly you progress.

Your motivation plays an important role too: a positive attitude and genuine interest in English will fuel your engagement and accelerate your learning journey.

IDIOMS IN POPULAR MEDIA: YOUR KEY TO FLUENT ENGLISH

Learning a new language is an incredible mental adventure. Grammar books provide the map, vocabulary gives you the tools, but idioms help you sound like a native speaker. Idioms are colorful phrases that might seem strange and not make sense but add flavor and personality to conversations.

To master these unique expressions, you need to hear them spoken—this is important. Reading them isn't enough; you must experience them in their natural environment.

Idioms communicate complex ideas efficiently, like talking about "cold feet" or "pulling someone's leg." These phrases have nothing to do with actual temperature or physical actions! Scientists find idioms fascinating because they show how our brains process language. We understand idioms as complete ideas rather than individual words requiring translation. They function as mental shortcuts.

POPULAR MEDIA: YOUR IDIOM MASTERCLASS

Movies, TV shows, music, and social media show how people speak. Think of them as your personal gateway to learning idioms in the most engaging way! Choose What You Love: Learning flows naturally when you're having fun. Pick genres you enjoy, whether sitcoms, drama, pop songs, podcasts, or audiobooks.

- **Use Subtitles**: in your native language (never English) because if you don't understand the spoken word, how could you understand the written word? Using subtitles in your native language will ensure that you understand.

- **Think Context:** Pay attention to who uses an idiom, when, and why. Is it playful? Sarcastic? Understanding this helps you use idioms appropriately.

- **Idiom Notebook:** Create your personal phrase book! Write down each idiom, its meaning, and an example from shows or songs.

- **Use Pen and Paper:** Writing in a physical notebook with a pen differs from typing on a computer. Using a pen in a notebook requires more effort and time. That physical act of writing helps embed idioms in your working memory, rather than letting them slip into long-term memory. It's like the famous idiom saying, "No pain, no gain."

- **Speak Like Natives:** Practice mimicking native speakers' speech patterns. This critical exercise trains both your mouth muscles for pronunciation and your ears for natural intonation.

- **Online Resources:** Explore websites and apps dedicated to idioms. They offer engaging explanations, quizzes, and exercises. Commit to just 15 minutes of practice daily—make it part of your routine.

The English language has nearly 25,000 idioms. While this might seem overwhelming, remembering and mastering even 100 common idioms will make your speech much more natural. Remember, the more you engage with English, the easier it becomes. This famous idiom perfectly illustrates this: "Rome wasn't built in a day." Similarly, your knowledge of idioms won't develop in a day. Take it one step at a time; soon, you'll know enough of them to add color to your English.

Now, let's dive into some practical examples to clarify this. Imagine you're watching a popular TV show like Friends. In one episode, Joey says, "I'm on the edge of my seat!"

If you're new to idioms, this might sound confusing—why is Joey sitting on the edge of his chair? But with context, you'll realize he's excited or interested in what's happening. This is how idioms work—they paint a picture that goes beyond the literal meaning of the words.

Here's another example: You're listening to a Taylor Swift song, and she sings, "I'm feeling under the weather." If you didn't know this idiom, you might think she's literally under the sky or rain. But in reality, it means she's feeling sick or unwell. By paying attention to these phrases in songs, shows, or movies, you'll recognize and understand them naturally.

STEP-BY-STEP BREAKDOWN

1. **Watch a Scene or Listen to a Song**: Choose something you enjoy. For example, watch a scene from "The Office" or listen to a song by "Ed Sheeran."

2. **Identify the Idiom**: When you hear a phrase that doesn't make literal sense, like "break the ice" or "hit the sack," pause and take note.

3. **Look it Up**: Use an idiom dictionary or an online resource to find the meaning. For example, "break the ice" means to start a conversation in a social setting, and "hit the sack" means to go to bed.

4. **Write it Down**: Add it to your idiom notebook with the meaning and an example sentence.

For instance:

1. **Break the ice:** "At the party, I told a joke to break the ice."

2. **Hit the sack:** "I'm so tired; I'm going to hit the sack early tonight."

Practice: Try using the idiom in your own sentences. For example, "I always feel nervous at networking events, but I try to break the ice by asking about people's hobbies."

Here's a Challenge: Pick a movie or TV show you love and watch it with subtitles in your native language. Every time you hear an idiom, write it down and research its meaning. Then, try to use it in a conversation or write a short story using that idiom. For example, if you hear "spill the beans" (which means to reveal a secret), you could write: "I accidentally spilled the beans about the surprise party, and now everyone knows!"

Remember, the key is consistency. Even if you learn just one idiom a day, you'll know 90 idioms in three months! That's enough to make your English sound much more natural and fluent. And don't worry if you make mistakes—native speakers misuse idioms sometimes too. The important thing is to keep practicing.

As you continue this journey, you'll notice how idioms pop up everywhere—in conversations, advertisements, and news headlines.

For example, you might see a headline like "Company Hits the Jackpot with New Product." Now you know it doesn't mean they literally won the lottery; it means they achieved great success.

So, grab your notebook, pick your favorite show or song, and explore the colorful world of idioms. Before you know it, you'll use them like a native English speaker.

CHAPTER 3

NAVIGATING THE WORLD OF ENGLISH VARIETIES

The evolution of English is a fascinating journey spanning centuries. You might wonder why English has been spreading globally for so long—since the 16th century, primarily through British colonial expansion. This worldwide reach continued as colonies adopted English as their official language, and the rise of the United States as a global superpower in the 20th century further accelerated English's influence through cultural exports and economic dominance.

Today, English primarily exists in two primary forms: British and American. While other regional varieties exist, they're based on one of these two standards. Contrary to what many assume, British English speakers outnumber American English speakers globally by about seven to one.

This surprising fact often shocks my students when I share it during class! Rajiv, a software developer from India, once told me, "I always thought American English was more common because of Hollywood movies. Learning that British English dominates globally changed how I approached my studies."

This revelation helped him understand why certain English expressions were more recognized internationally than others.

GEOGRAPHIC DISTRIBUTION: A WORLD DIVIDED BY VOCABULARY

The geographic distribution of these variants creates an interesting linguistic map:

British English Dominates in:

- All of Africa (from Nigeria to South Africa)

- Most of Asia (including the population giants China and India)

- Australia and New Zealand

- Much of Europe (particularly in educational settings)

- **American English Dominates in:**

- North and South America (from Canada to Brazil)

- Specific European countries (Germany and Turkey show a strong preference)

- Israel (in the Middle East)

- South Korea and Japan (in Asia, largely because of post-WWII American influence)

Vinka, a High School teacher from Brazil, said, "In Brazil, we naturally adopt American English, but when I had new students who had recently emigrated from Africa, I realized I also needed to understand British expressions and was surprised with the many differences between American and British English."

DIFFERENCES IN VOCABULARY: BRITISH VS. AMERICAN ENGLISH

The biggest difference between American and British English is their vocabulary and spelling for the same word. While both versions of the language share the same basic grammar and structure, they often have different words for the same things and the spelling of many exact words is different. These differences in vocabulary and spelling can make American and British English sound more than slightly different. These variations have developed due to historical, cultural, and geographical influences.

Despite these differences, American and British English are still very much the same language at their core.

Here are classic examples that confuse learners:

- British **"lift"** vs. American **"elevator"**

- British **"flat"** vs. American **"apartment"**

- British **"lorry"** vs. American **"truck"**

- British **"queue"** vs. American **"line"**

- British **"holiday"** vs. American **"vacation"**

Some words have dramatically different meanings across these varieties of English, which can lead to awkward situations:

"Pants" means underwear in British English but outerwear in American English.

"Braces" refers to suspenders in British English but orthodontic devices in American English.

"Chips" means French fries in British English but thin crisps in American English.

"Biscuit" describes a sweet cookie in British English but a savory bread roll in American English.

Ahmad, an engineering student from Saudi Arabia, once told our class about asking for "pants" for himself in a London department store when he meant trousers.

The sales assistant's face turned so red she thought he wanted to buy ladies' underwear!

"Now I always remember which words have different meanings across the Atlantic," he laughed.

SPELLING DIFFERENCES: EXTRA LETTERS AND FLIPPED ENDINGS

Beyond vocabulary, spelling differences reveal which version of English you're reading:

- British English includes the letter "u" in words like **"colour,"** **"favour,"** and **"humour,"** while American English drops it: **"color," "favor," "humor."**

- British English uses **"-re"** in words like **"centre"** and **"theatre,"** while American English uses **"-er"**: **"center," "theater."**

- British English maintains **"-ise"** endings in words like **"organize,"** while American English uses **"-ize"**: **"organize."**

- British English doubles the final "l" in words like **"traveller,"** while American English uses a single "l": **"traveler."**

As my French-Canadian student Megan once joked, "I feel like I'm in a spelling identity crisis—we use some British spelling and some American. Canada is the only English-speaking country in the world to mix both versions of English. It's the perfect metaphor for being Canadian!"

GRAMMAR AND PUNCTUATION: IMPORTANT DIFFERENCES

The differences extend beyond vocabulary and spelling to grammar and punctuation:

- British English often uses present perfect tense (**"I have eaten"**), whereas American English uses simple past (**"I ate."**)

- Collective nouns like (**"team"**) take plural verbs in British English (**"The team are winning"**) but singular verbs in American English (**"The team is winning."**)

- British English uses single quotation marks first (**'like this'**) while American English uses double quotation marks (**"like this"**).

Carlos, an editor at a Spanish international publishing company, developed his "English schizophrenia checklist"—a document to help him keep track of which version he was writing for different clients. "The hardest part is staying consistent," he told me.

PRONUNCIATION: MORE THAN JUST ACCENTS

While we'll explore accents in more depth later, it's worth noting that British and American English differ in pronunciation patterns:

- British English rarely pronounces **"r"** sounds unless followed by a vowel, while American English pronounces all **"r"** sounds.

- Words like "schedule" begin with **"sh"** in British English but **"sk"** in American English.

- Words like "privacy" emphasize different syllables: **"PRIV-acy"** in British English versus **"pri-VA-cy"** in American English.

IMPORTANCE OF UNDERSTANDING BOTH VARIETIES

In our increasingly connected world, understanding both American and British English has become essential for effective communication. As English continues its role as a global language, we regularly encounter both varieties in professional and personal contexts, making familiarity with their distinct features increasingly valuable.

Knowing both varieties can help you navigate countless situations, from international business meetings to studying abroad or enjoying media from different English-speaking regions.

Simple awareness that Americans say **"elevator"** while Brits say **"lift,"** or that Americans write **"color"** while Brits include the letter **"u"** in **"colour"** can prevent confusion in your daily communications.

Li Wei, a Chinese business executive I tutored, once shared a story about a conference call disaster in which she kept talking about "tables." At the same time, her British colleagues repeatedly mentioned "charts." After fifteen frustrating minutes, everyone realized they were discussing the same thing—data visualizations! Now, I prepare a mental British-American translation guide before international meetings," she laughed.

CULTURAL AWARENESS AND ADAPTATION

Adapting your language to your audience shows cultural awareness and respect. Using the preferred variety of English when talking to American or British colleagues, clients, or friends helps build stronger relationships and creates meaningful cultural connections.

Martina, an Italian fashion designer who worked with clients in New York and London, became masterful at code-switching between varieties.

"When speaking with Americans, I talk about fall collections and pants, but with the British team, it's autumn collections and trousers, she explained. "It's not just about vocabulary; you want to show respect for their cultural identity, too."

Learning both varieties of English also exposes you to a broader vocabulary and more colorful expressions. This flexibility lets you express yourself more clearly and creatively in any scenario. Being familiar with both varieties of English is like having access to two rich toolboxes instead of one. Why hold yourself back when you can use both.

MASTERING BOTH VARIETIES

To master both American and British English:

1. **Identify Variety:** If you plan to study in Britain or work with British companies, focus on British English. If your connections are primarily American, focus there first.

2. **Be Consistent**: Lukas, a German student studying engineering in England, learned the hard way after submitting a university paper with mixed spellings, "My professor circled every instance where I switched between British and American spelling. Now I

always check document settings to maintain consistency."

3. **Create a Personal Reference Guide**: Record the differences you encounter regularly in your field or interests.

4. **Balance Media**: Alternate between American shows like "Friends" and British shows like "The Crown."

5. **Label New Vocabulary**: Note whether they're primarily British or American when learning new words.

Alexandra, a Greek marketing professional, created color-coded flashcards—blue for British terms and red for American. "This simple system helped me track which words belonged to which English," she explained. "I can now confidently adapt my language depending on which client I'm speaking with."

EMBRACING LINGUISTIC FLEXIBILITY

The most valuable approach may be developing comfort with both varieties while supporting consistency when appropriate. María, a Spanish executive who works with global teams, summed it up brilliantly: "I think of it like knowing how to use both chopsticks and a fork, different tools for different situations, but both get food to your mouth!"

CHAPTER 4

MASTERING ENGLISH THROUGH PODCASTS AND AUDIOBOOKS

Learning English need not be boring or stressful. It can be fun, relaxing, and highly effective when you use the right tools.

Podcasts and audiobooks are two of the best resources available to help you improve your English skills, especially your listening abilities. Let's dive into how these tools can transform your English learning journey.

WHY PODCASTS AND AUDIOBOOKS

They are powerful learning tools. They provide a relaxed and enjoyable way to immerse yourself in English. Unlike traditional classroom learning, podcasts and audiobooks let you learn at your own pace, in your own time, and in a way that fits your lifestyle.

One of the most significant advantages is their convenience. You can listen to them anywhere and anytime—while commuting, exercising, cooking, or relaxing at home. This makes them perfect for busy individuals who want to improve their English without adding extra stress to their schedules.

THE BENEFITS OF LISTENING TO AUDIOBOOKS

Audiobooks, in particular, offer unique benefits for English learners. Here's why they are so effective:

1. **Improve Listening Skills:** Listening to audiobooks helps you get used to English's natural rhythm, pronunciation, and intonation. Over time, you'll find it easier to understand native speakers, even when they babble.

2. **Expand Vocabulary:** Audiobooks expose you to a wide range of words and phrases in context. This makes learning new vocabulary and understanding how to use it correctly in sentences easier.

3. **Enhance Pronunciation:** You can learn how to pronounce words accurately by listening to professional narrators. You can even pause and repeat sections to practice your pronunciation.

4. **Boost Comprehension:** Audiobooks often include expressive narration, which helps you understand the emotions and meanings behind the words. This improves your overall understanding of the language.

5. **Gradually Increase Level:** Audiobooks are a powerful resource for your English learning journey, whether you're a beginner or an advanced learner.

You can start your audiobook journey with the Recall Total English audiobook version and then gradually move to more challenging books as your skills improve.

HOW TO GET STARTED

Choose topics or genres that interest you: This will keep you motivated and make learning fun rather than a chore. For beginners, look for audiobooks with simple language or those specifically designed for English learners. As you progress, you can explore more complex materials.

Remember, Consistency is Key: Listening for just 15–20 minutes daily can make a big difference over time. So, grab your headphones and find an audiobook you love.

THE BENEFITS OF LISTENING TO PODCASTS

Listening to English language podcasts is an excellent way for new learners to improve their listening skills and vocabulary.

Here's how:

1. Improve Listening Skills

Listening to podcasts helps learners get used to the language's sounds, rhythm, and speed. At first, it might be hard to understand everything, but with time, learners will notice they can catch more words and phrases. This is called "training the ear."

Start with podcasts that speak slowly and clearly, like those for English learners. As you get better, you can try podcasts on topics you enjoy, even if they are for native speakers.

2. Builds Vocabulary

Podcasts cover many topics so learners can hear new words in different contexts. More importantly, learners can choose topics that interest them.

3. Teaches Natural English

Often use everyday language, slang, and expressions common in real-life conversations. This helps learners sound more natural when they speak. Pay attention to how speakers use phrases like "by the way," "actually," or "you know." These are common in casual English.

4. Improves Pronunciation

By listening to native speakers, learners can copy how they pronounce words and sentences. This helps with speaking clearly and correctly.

5. Makes Learning Fun

Podcasts are interesting because they discuss real-life topics like news, stories, or hobbies. This makes learning feel less like studying and more like entertainment.

6. Strengthen Focus

Listening to podcasts requires concentration, which helps learners practice focusing on English for more extended periods. This is useful for understanding conversations in real-life.

7. Convenient and Flexible

It can be listened to anytime, anywhere—while commuting, cooking, or relaxing. This makes it easy to practice English daily.

8. Exposes Learners to Different Accents

Often feature speakers from different countries, so learners can get used to hearing different English accents like American, British, or Australian.

9. Encourages Active Listening

Some podcasts have exercises or questions for listeners to think about. This helps learners practice active listening, focusing on understanding and remembering what they hear.

10. Boosts Confidence

Learners will feel more confident in their English skills as they understand and learn new words. This confidence can help them speak more freely in real-life situations.

CONCLUSION

Podcasts and audiobooks provide an enjoyable and effective way to enhance your English skills. Choose content that excites you, listen actively, and review regularly.

You'll significantly improve your English by following these guidelines and practicing consistently.

EXERCISE

Find an engaging podcast or audiobook and spend 30 minutes listening actively. While you listen, write down any new words, interesting phrases, or expressions you hear.

Practice your pronunciation and speaking rhythm by repeating after the speakers, mimicking their tone and intonation patterns. This exercise helps train your ear while building your vocabulary and natural speaking ability.

CHAPTER 5

READING WORD BY WORD VS. FULL SENTENCES

When you read in English, do you focus on each word individually rather than understanding the overall meaning of the text? If so, you're not alone.

Many language learners, especially those in the early stages of learning English, tend to read word by word. While this approach might seem logical initially, it is challenging to understand the entire text, as the brain is not processing whole sentences.

WHY DO WE FOCUS ON INDIVIDUAL WORDS

When learning a new language, focusing on individual words is natural. After all, building vocabulary is an important part of language acquisition. You might need to understand every word to ensure you're not missing anything. However, this approach can become a barrier as you progress. Reading word by word slows you down, disrupts the text flow, and prevents you from seeing the bigger picture.

For example, consider the sentence: "The sun was gleaming in the clear blue sky." If you focus on each word individually, you might think about the meanings of "sun," "gleaming," "clear," and "blue." But if you don't consider how these words work together, you might miss the overall meaning—that the sentence describes a beautiful, sunny day. This is why reading sentence by sentence is far more effective than reading word by word.

CONSEQUENCES OF FOCUSING ON INDIVIDUAL WORDS

1. **Reduced Understanding:** Focusing on individual words might miss the text's meaning. You could overlook critical details like the main idea, supporting points, or the author's tone and intent.

2. **Increased Cognitive Load:** Reading word by word is mentally exhausting. It requires more effort to process each word individually, leading to fatigue, decreased motivation, and even frustration.

3. **Limited Engagement:** If you are too focused on individual words, you might not fully engage with the material. You could miss the emotional impact of a story, the logic of an argument, or the beauty of a well-crafted sentence.

WHY TRANSLATION IS PROBLEMATIC

When you translate English text into your native language, you're trying to fit one language's structure, idioms, and culture into another. This often leads to misunderstandings. Like any language, English has unique expressions, phrases, and cultural references that don't always have the same meaning in other languages. For example, consider the idiom "It's raining cats and dogs."

If you translate this word for word, you might imagine literal animals falling from the sky, which is not the intended meaning. The phrase means that it's raining heavily.

By translating it, you miss the idiom's true meaning and the colorful way English speakers describe weather.

Similarly, English often uses metaphors, phrasal verbs, and colloquial expressions that don't translate well. For example, "let the cat out of the bag" doesn't involve actual cats or bags—it means revealing a secret. If you try to translate this phrase word for word, you'll end up confused and miss the point entirely. This is why relying on translation can lead to not understanding the text.

THE RISK OF LOSING THE CONTEXT

One of the biggest challenges of translation is that it often strips away the context. English has words and phrases with emotions and cultural significance. For example, "home" doesn't just mean a physical place to live—it can mean feelings of comfort, belonging, and nostalgia. If you translate it into your native language, you might lose these emotional layers and have a flat, literal meaning.

The word "run" can mean moving quickly on foot, managing something (like a business), or even describing the operation of a machine (like a car).

The meaning depends entirely on the context in which it's used. If you translate it without considering the context, you might misinterpret its meaning entirely.

THE BENEFITS OF THINKING IN ENGLISH

To master English, it's essential to think in the language rather than relying on translation.

Here's why:

1. **Improved Fluency:** When you think in English, you process the language more naturally and quickly. This helps you speak and

write more fluently, as you're not constantly translating in your head.

2. **Better Comprehension:** By focusing on the meaning of the text rather than individual words, you'll develop a deeper understanding of the material. You'll also be better equipped to pick up on idioms, metaphors, and cultural references.

3. **Cultural Awareness:** Language and culture are deeply intertwined. Thinking in English will help you better understand English-speaking cultures, including their values, humor, and ways of expressing ideas.

HOW TO STOP TRANSLATING AND START THINKING IN ENGLISH

Breaking the habit of translation takes time and practice, but it's well worth the effort.

Here are practical strategies to help you make the shift:

1. **Immerse Yourself in English:** Surround yourself with English as much as possible. Watch movies, listen to podcasts, read books, and engage in conversations in English. The more exposure you have, the easier it will be to think in the language.

2. **Use Context to Guess Meaning:** Instead of reaching for a dictionary whenever you encounter an unfamiliar word, try to guess its meaning based on the context. This will help you develop your intuition and reduce your reliance on translation.

3. **Practice Active Reading:** As you read, focus on understanding the text's overall meaning rather than translating individual words. Ask yourself questions like, "What is the author trying to say?" or "How does this sentence connect to the previous one?"

4. **Think in English Daily:** Challenge yourself to think in English throughout the day. For example, when making a grocery list, try to

write it in English. Or, when you're reflecting on your day, describe it to yourself in English.

5. **Learn Idioms and Phrases:** Familiarize yourself with common English idioms, phrasal verbs, and expressions. Understanding these will help you avoid literal translations and understand the text's true meaning.

6. **Speak and Write in English:** Practice speaking and writing in English as often as possible. This will help you reduce your dependence on translation.

CONCLUSION

While translating English text into your native language might feel like a helpful shortcut, it can slow your progress and prevent you from fully understanding the language. You'll improve your fluency, understanding, and cultural awareness by avoiding translation and learning to think in English. Remember, language learning is not just about memorizing words—it's about understanding how those words come together to convey meaning, emotion, and ideas. So, take the leap, immerse yourself in English, and start thinking in the language. You'll be amazed at how much more natural and enjoyable the learning process becomes!

CHAPTER 6

THE POWER OF PRACTICING SPOKEN ENGLISH

Let's talk about the second most important part of learning English: speaking. Being able to speak English is key to communicating effectively with others.

It's also closely connected to your listening skills—after all, you need to understand what others are saying to respond correctly.

Speaking English is much more than simply pronouncing words the right way. It's about clearly and confidently sharing your thoughts, ideas, and feelings with others.

It's about:

Improve your Listening Skills: The more you practice speaking, the more you'll improve your listening skills. This is because speaking and listening are closely related, and when you practice speaking, you're also practicing your ability to understand spoken English.

Build Confidence: Speaking English can be intimidating, especially if you're not used to it. However, the more you practice, the more confident you'll become. This confidence will translate to other areas of your life, such as work, social interactions, and personal relationships.

USING TECHNOLOGY TO YOUR ADVANTAGE

With technology, endless resources are available to empower you to practice spoken English. From video applications to interactive software to AI, consider these tools as part of your practice routine:

Speech Recognition Software: Tools like Google Voice or language learning apps often use speech recognition technology. They can provide immediate feedback on your pronunciation and clarity, allowing for targeted improvement.

Games and Interactive Platforms: Language games that require speaking can make learning more enjoyable.

INCORPORATING ENGLISH INTO YOUR DAILY LIFE

Think in English: Try translating your thoughts into English as you go about your day. Whether you're planning your schedule or wondering what to cook for dinner, thinking in English can strengthen your speaking ability.

Label your Environment: Consider labeling objects around your house with English names. Every time you see an item, say its name aloud. This constant exposure can reinforce vocabulary creatively.

THE LIMITATIONS OF PRACTICING SPOKEN ENGLISH

While practicing spoken English is essential, many learners face limitations. If you live in a country where English is not widely spoken or work in an environment where English is not commonly used, finding opportunities to practice speaking is challenging.

Also, enrolling in online services that provide English-speaking tutors can be costly, especially if you want to practice for more than an hour a week.

COMPLEMENTING YOUR SPEAKING
PRACTICE WITH READING ALOUD

So, how can you complement your speaking practice without spending much money? The answer is simple: reading aloud. When you read text aloud, your brain considers it more like speaking than reading.

This is because reading aloud involves using your vocal cords, tongue, and lips to produce sounds just like you would when speaking. Reading aloud is an effective way to practice speaking because it engages your brain more actively than when you read silently. Reading silently just inputs data into your brain; no learning process is involved.

Reading aloud helps you become more aware of your pronunciation, intonation, and rhythm, essential elements of effective communication. By hearing yourself speak, you can find areas where you struggle, such as difficult words or phrases, and work on improving them. This self-awareness is a key step in refining your speaking skills and building confidence in your ability to express yourself clearly.

Another benefit of reading aloud is that it lets you practice at your own pace. Unlike conversations, where you might feel pressured to respond quickly, reading aloud will enable you to pause, repeat, and focus on specific words or sentences.

This controlled environment is ideal for beginners or those anxious about speaking to others. Over time, this practice can help you develop fluency and reduce hesitation when engaging in real-life conversations.

Choose materials that interest you and match your language

level to maximize your reading aloud practice. For example, you could read articles, short stories, poems, or even movie script dialogues.

Incorporating reading aloud into your daily routine can also enhance your listening skills. As you read, try to mimic the tone and rhythm of native speakers by listening carefully to audio recordings or videos.

Reading aloud is a simple, cost-effective, and highly effective way to complement your speaking practice. This technique can help you become a more fluent and articulate communicator by engaging multiple senses, improving pronunciation, and building confidence. So, grab a book, an article, or any text that inspires you, and start reading aloud today!

CONCLUSION

Practicing spoken English is a fundamental skill for effective communication. By using a combination of reading aloud, language partnerships, technology, and real-life integration, you can build an intense practice routine that enhances your speaking abilities and nurtures your confidence.

Remember, every effort counts, and the more you invest in your practice, the closer you will get to achieving fluency.

EXERCISE

1. **Pick Something Interesting to Read:** news articles, blogs, or books. This will help you stay motivated and engaged.

2. **Start at Slow Pace:** gradually go faster as you feel more at ease.

3. **Record Yourself:** Read aloud and record yourself, then listen to

what you recorded. This will help you find ways to improve.

4. **Practice Regularly:** Read aloud consistently, even for a few minutes daily.

Remember to pay attention to your pronunciation, intonation, and fluency as you practice.

CHAPTER 7

UNLOCKING THE POWER OF AI FOR ENGLISH LANGUAGE LEARNING

In today's fast-paced, technology-driven world, AI's a new game-changer. AI is transforming the way we learn languages, offering personalized, interactive, and accessible tools that can revolutionize your English language learning journey. Let's dive into the exciting world of AI and discover how it can help you master English more efficiently and effectively.

THE RISE OF AI IN LANGUAGE LEARNING

AI has made significant strides in recent years, and its applications in education are nothing short of revolutionary. AI-powered tools like ChatGPT, Gemini, Claude, and Ninja are designed to help learners develop their English skills in once unimaginable ways. These AI assistants can simulate real-life conversations, provide instant feedback, and adapt to your individual learning needs, making them invaluable resources for learners of all levels.

PERSONALIZED LEARNING AT YOUR FINGERTIPS

One of the most significant benefits of using AI for English language learning is its ability to offer personalized experiences. Unlike traditional classroom settings where one-size-fits-all approaches are standard, AI tools can analyze your strengths, weaknesses, and learning pace to create tailored lesson plans. For example, if you struggle with grammar but excel in vocabulary, an AI assistant can focus on providing targeted grammar exercises while still challenging your vocabulary skills. This customization level ensures you're always working on areas that need improvement, maximizing your learning efficiency.

24/7 ACCESSIBILITY AND CONVENIENCE

AI-powered language learning tools are available anytime, anywhere. Whether on your morning commute, taking a break at work, or winding down at home, you can access AI assistants to practice your English. This flexibility eliminates the need for rigid schedules or physical classrooms, letting you learn at your own pace and on your own terms. Plus, with AI, you need not wait for a teacher's availability—instant feedback and support are just a click away.

INTERACTIVE AND ENGAGING PRACTICE

AI assistants can engage you in realistic conversations, role-playing scenarios, and even games that make practicing English enjoyable. For example, you can simulate a job interview, order food at a restaurant, or debate a topic with an AI partner that responds naturally and helps you refine your skills. This immersive experience boosts your confidence and prepares you for real-world interactions.

INSTANT FEEDBACK AND ERROR CORRECTION

One of the most challenging parts of learning a language is identifying and correcting mistakes. AI tools excel in this area by providing instant feedback on your pronunciation, grammar, and sentence structure. For example, if you mispronounce a word or use incorrect grammar, an AI assistant can immediately point out the error and suggest corrections. This real time feedback speeds up your learning process and helps you avoid forming bad habits.

EXPANDING VOCABULARY AND CULTURAL KNOWLEDGE

AI-powered tools can also help you expand your vocabulary and deepen your understanding of English-speaking cultures. Many AI assistants have vast databases of words, phrases, and idioms, letting you learn new expressions in context.

BUILDING CONFIDENCE THROUGH PRACTICE

For many learners, speaking English can be intimidating, especially in front of others. AI offers a safe and judgment-free environment to practice speaking without fear of embarrassment. You can have as many conversations as you need, repeat exercises until you feel confident, and track your progress. This consistent practice builds your confidence and prepares you for real-life interactions with native speakers.

COST EFFECTIVE LEARNING SOLUTIONS

Traditional language courses and private tutors can be expensive, making them inaccessible for many learners. AI-powered tools are often more affordable or even free.

THE FUTURE OF ENGLISH LANGUAGE LEARNING

As AI technology continues to evolve, its potential for language learning is limitless. Future advancements may include more sophisticated conversational abilities, enhanced cultural insights, and seamless integration with other technologies like virtual (VR) and augmented reality (AR). These innovations will further enhance the learning experience, making it more immersive, engaging, and effective.

THE BENEFITS OF USING AI FOR ENGLISH LANGUAGE LEARNING

AI assistants can help learners in many ways:

1. **Personalized Learning:** AI assistants can tailor their responses to the learner's level, interests, and learning style, providing a personalized learning experience.

2. **Instant Feedback**: AI assistants can offer instant feedback on grammar, pronunciation, and vocabulary usage, helping learners improve.

3. **Conversational Practice**: AI assistants can engage in conversations with learners, providing an opportunity to practice speaking and listening skills realistically and interactively.

4. **Access to Authentic Materials**: AI assistants can give learners authentic materials, such as news articles, videos, and podcasts, to help them develop their reading, listening, and comprehension skills.

THE BEST AI ASSISTANTS FOR ENGLISH LANGUAGE LEARNING

While many AI assistants are available, some stand out for their features and capabilities. Gemini and Ninja are two examples of AI assistants that offer advanced features, such as:

1. **Text-to-Speech**: Gemini can read back its responses, allowing learners to practice their listening skills and pronunciation.

2. **Speech-to-Text**: Gemini and Ninja let learners use a microphone to speak to them, allowing them to practice speaking to the AI.

HOW AI ASSISTANTS CAN HELP LEARNERS WITH GRAMMAR

1. **Grammar and Vocabulary Practice**: A learner can ask an AI assistant to explain a grammar rule or provide examples of vocabulary usage. The AI assistant can explain and suggest exercises to help practice the idea.

Example: Learner: "Can you explain the difference between affect and effect?"

AI assistant: "The words affect, and effect are often confused but have different meanings. Affect is a verb that means to influence or have an impact on something, while effect is a noun that refers to the result of a particular action. For example, The rain will affect the crops' versus The effect of the rain on the crops was devastating."

2. **Conversational Practice**: A learner can engage in a conversation with an AI assistant, practicing their speaking and listening skills realistically and interactively.

Example: Learner: "Hello, how are you?"

AI assistant: "Hello! I'm doing well, thank you. How about you?"

Learner: "I'm good, thanks. I'm planning a trip to New York City. Can you recommend any restaurants?"

AI assistant: "New York City has many successful restaurants. Have you considered trying some of the classic New York-style pizza places, like Lombardi's or Joe's Pizza?"

PAID VS. FREE VERSIONS

While free versions of AI assistants can be helpful, paid versions often offer more advanced features and better results. Paid versions may include:

1. **Unlimited conversations:** Paid versions typically offer unlimited conversations, allowing learners to practice their speaking and listening skills without worries of set limits.

2. **Advanced feedback**: Paid versions may offer more detailed feedback on grammar, pronunciation, and vocabulary usage.

CONCLUSION

AI assistants can help learners develop their English skills more efficiently by providing personalized learning experiences, instant feedback, and conversational practice. While free versions can be helpful, paid versions often offer more advanced features and better results. I recommend exploring the paid versions of these AI assistants to unlock their full potential.

EXERCISE

Try using an AI assistant like Gemini or Ninja to practice your English skills. Ask them to explain a grammar rule, provide examples of vocabulary usage, or engage in a conversation. Use their text-to-speech and speech-to-text features to practice your listening and speaking skills.

CHAPTER 8

LEARNING ENGLISH THROUGH INTERACTIVE VIDEO GAMES

In earlier chapters, we explored how movies, TV shows, podcasts, audiobooks, and AI can help you improve your English. Now, let's discover how video games and other interactive media can become powerful tools for language development.

WHY VIDEO GAMES AND INTERACTIVE MEDIA?

Video games create an immersive environment where you participate rather than passively consume content. This engagement makes learning more effective and memorable.

When you play games in English, you:

1. **Learn in Context**: You understand new vocabulary and expressions through meaningful interactions.

2. **Practice Decision-Making**: You must quickly understand instructions and dialogue to progress.

3. **Repeat Naturally**: Games encourage repetition without feeling like boring practice.

4. **Receive Immediate Feedback**: Games tell you right away if you've understood correctly.

TYPES OF GAMES AND THEIR LANGUAGE BENEFITS

Different games offer various language learning opportunities:

Story-Based Games: Games like "Life is Strange," "The Walking Dead," or "Detroit: Become Human" feature-rich narratives with extensive dialogue.

These games often include conversation choices, helping you understand different ways to express the same idea in English.

Multiplayer Online Games: Games such as "Fortnite," "Minecraft," or "Among Us" connect you with English speakers worldwide. These games require real time communication, pushing you to understand and respond quickly — like in real conversations.

Puzzle and Word Games: Apps like "Words with Friends," "Scrabble," or "Wordscapes" directly target vocabulary building. These games challenge you to recall and actively use English words.

HOW TO LEARN EFFECTIVELY THROUGH GAMING

Follow these tips to maximize your learning:

5. **Play with Subtitles:** Match what you hear with what you read to improve understanding.

6. **Take Screenshots of Useful Language**: Capture new vocabulary or phrases to review later.

7. **Join English-Speaking Communities**: take part in forums, Discord servers, or subreddits related to your favorite games to practice your English in authentic discussions.

8. **Record Yourself**: Try commenting on your gameplay in English, like popular streamers do.

9. **Balance Game Types**: Mix entertainment-focused games with more educational ones.

BEYOND TRADITIONAL VIDEO GAMES

Other interactive media can also boost your English skills:

10. **Virtual reality experiences**: VR applications can simulate real-life conversations.

11. **Interactive stories**: Apps like "Episode" or "Choices" let you influence storylines while exposing you to conversational English.

12. **Social media challenges**: Participate in English-speaking discussions on TikTok, Facebook, or Instagram.

A SUCCESS STORY

Let me share a story about my student, Alex, an IT technician from Russia. When he started learning English, his vocabulary was limited, and his pronunciation was hard to understand. But Alex loved playing online games.

I encouraged him to join English-speaking game platforms and use voice chat. At first, he was nervous and only listened to others. Gradually, he began using simple phrases like "Need help here" or "Let's go this way." As time passed, his confidence grew.

Six months later, Alex spoke with players from America, Britain, and Australia. He picked up slang, idioms, and even jokes you won't find in any textbook. He developed the confidence to speak without worrying about making mistakes.

GETTING STARTED TODAY

Begin with these simple steps:

13. **Choose a game you already enjoy**: If possible, switch the language to English.

14. **Start with a comfortable difficulty level**: Make sure you understand the basic instructions.

15. **Keep a gaming vocabulary journal**: Write new words and phrases you encounter.

Remember that the goal is both learning and enjoyment. If a game feels too challenging language-wise, try something simpler first. As your skills improve, you can challenge yourself with more complex games and interactions.

Incorporating video games and interactive media into your English learning routine will help you develop practical language skills in an engaging, low-pressure environment.

This approach will also help you build the confidence you need for real-world conversations.

CHAPTER 9

BUILDING CONFIDENCE — THE KEY TO SPEAKING ENGLISH FLUENTLY

In earlier chapters, we explored various media for improving your English skills—from movies and TV shows to podcasts, audiobooks, AI, and video games. Now, let's address something equally important but often overlooked: confidence.

WHY CONFIDENCE MATTERS

Many English learners face this common problem: they perform well on written tests or while reading but fall apart when it's time to speak.

María, a chemical engineer from Brazil, illustrates this perfectly. On paper, her English was nearly flawless. She could write essays with sophisticated vocabulary and correct grammar. However, during meetings at her international company, she stumbles over basic sentences and forgets simple words. The problem wasn't her knowledge; it was her confidence.

THE CONFIDENCE PARADOX

This creates what I call the "confidence paradox" in language learning:

- You need to speak to improve your English.

- You avoid speaking because you lack confidence.

- Your speaking doesn't improve because you avoid it.

- Your confidence remains low because your speaking doesn't improve.

This cycle traps many learners at the same level for years. They continue studying more vocabulary and grammar, hoping it will somehow translate into speaking ability, but it rarely does without directly addressing confidence.

HOW LOW CONFIDENCE AFFECTS SPEAKING

When you lack confidence while speaking English, several things happen:

1. **Your Brain Freezes**: You know the words but can't access them quickly.

2. **Your Pronunciation Worsens**: Nervousness affects your mouth muscles and breathing.

3. **You Simplify Your Speech**: You use only basic words and phrases you feel safe with.

4. **You Speak Less**: You avoid situations where English is needed.

Even advanced learners can sound like beginners when anxiety takes over. Your throat tightens, your heart races, and the English you've studied for years vanishes from your memory.

MEDIA IMMERSION BUILDS CONFIDENCE

The good news is that the media-based approach we've

discussed throughout this book naturally builds confidence in several ways:

1. Familiar Patterns Become Automatic

Common phrases become deeply familiar when you regularly watch TV shows, listen to podcasts, or play games in English.

Your brain recognizes these patterns and can produce them automatically, even when you're nervous. This creates "safe zone words" — expressions you can say confidently, even in stressful situations.

2. Your Listening Develops Naturally

Immersion in English media trains your ear to recognize sounds, rhythms, and intonation patterns. This improved listening ability makes conversation less stressful because you understand others more efficiently, giving you more mental space to focus on your speaking.

3. You Absorb Cultural Context

Media introduces you to cultural ideas, jokes, and social expectations that textbooks often don't discuss. This understanding of culture makes you feel more like one of the group instead of a stranger when talking to native English speakers.

4. You Begin Thinking In English

Consuming media regularly can help you think in English instead of translating from your first language. This direct processing is much faster and creates a more confident speaking experience.

THE THOMAS STORY: FROM KNOWLEDGE TO CONFIDENCE

Thomas, a German engineer, came to me with an interesting

problem. He had studied English for 15 years and had an excellent understanding of grammar and vocabulary. He could read technical manuals and write professional emails very well. Yet, he would freeze up during international conference calls and struggle to express simple ideas. Thomas approached speaking English like an engineering problem—he constructed perfect sentences in his head before saying anything. This created awkward pauses and growing anxiety as he felt pressure to speak.

Instead of more grammar lessons, I prescribed a simple media routine:

5. Twenty minutes of English podcasts during his morning commute.

6. English YouTube videos during lunch breaks.

7. One episode of an English TV series (43 minutes) each evening.

8. Weekend video game play (60 minutes or more) in English.

After three months, Thomas hadn't learned many new words or grammar rules. What had changed was his automatic access to the English he already knew. Expressions from his favorite TV characters became part of his speech. The rhythm of the podcasts influenced his speaking rhythm. Most importantly, he stopped overthinking and started trusting his instincts. Six months later, Thomas confidently led international calls and even made jokes in English. His knowledge hadn't gone up dramatically, but his confidence had transformed.

PRACTICAL CONFIDENCE BUILDING EXERCISES

Here are practical ways to build your speaking confidence through media:

Shadow Speaking: Pause a video or podcast and repeat what you heard, matching the speaker's tone and rhythm. This strengthens memory and confidence in pronunciation.

Record Yourself: Summarize an episode or explain a game in English. Listen back and compare your speech to that of native speakers. This will help you identify specific areas for improvement.

Character Practice: Choose a character from a TV show or movie you enjoy and practice speaking like them. This creates emotional distance from your speaking anxiety.

Media Discussion Groups: Find or create a group where you discuss English movies, shows, or games. This provides a natural reason to speak about something you enjoy.

Gradual Challenge: Start with easy media and gradually increase difficulty. Success with more straightforward content builds confidence for more challenging material.

Remember that confidence grows gradually, not overnight. Each small success builds on earlier ones, creating momentum toward fluent, natural English speaking.

CONCLUSION:

The confidence cycle

By immersing yourself in English media you enjoy, you create a positive cycle:

- You enjoy English content regularly.

- Your understanding improves naturally.

- Small speaking successes build confidence.

- Increased confidence leads to more speaking.

- More speaking accelerates your improvement.

- Your enjoyment of English grows further.

This positive cycle replaces the confidence paradox we discussed earlier. Instead of avoiding English because of low confidence, you seek out English because it's become an enjoyable part of your life.

CHAPTER 10

UNDERSTANDING AND MANAGING YOUR ACCENT

Have you ever had this frustrating experience? You say something in perfect English grammar with all the correct vocabulary, but the person you're speaking to looks at you with confusion. You repeat yourself—still confused. Finally, you write down what you're saying, and they immediately understand. What happened? Usually, the answer is simple: your accent got in the way.

Despite its importance, accent change is often overlooked in English language teaching. Most language courses focus on grammar, vocabulary, and pronunciation, but they neglect to address accents.

This is because accents are often seen as a personal trait, and it's assumed that learners will naturally pick up the accents of native speakers. However, this is not always the case, and learners may struggle to adjust their accents without proper guidance.

WHY ACCENTS MATTER MORE THAN YOU THINK

Let me share a story about my student Dmitri, a software developer from Russia. Dmitri had excellent vocabulary and nearly perfect grammar. He could write English emails that sounded like they came from a native speaker.

But when he spoke in meetings with American colleagues, they often asked him to repeat himself or nodded politely while understanding little.

One day, Dmitri frustratedly confessed: "I studied English for fifteen years. I know thousands of words. But when I order coffee, they don't understand me. A beginner student who can barely make a sentence but has a clearer accent gets their order right the first time!"

This story highlights an uncomfortable truth: when it comes to spoken communication, "how" you say something often matters more than "what" you say. Your accent can become an invisible barrier between your thoughts and your listener's understanding.

THE FRIED CHICKEN INCIDENT

I'll never forget my Chinese student Lian, a schoolteacher, and what later became known as "The Fried Chicken Incident." It perfectly illustrates why the Recall Total English method focuses so much on pronunciation and accent in real-world communication.

Lian was one of my best students. She had an impressive vocabulary and could write and read very well. Her grammar tests were nearly perfect. But like many English learners, she struggled with specific pronunciation patterns that didn't exist in her native Mandarin.

The English "fl" sound and the distinction between short and long vowels were challenging for her. This created what linguists call "interference patterns," where the brain applies native language rules to a new language.

One day in class, Lian asked if she could share a story with me, and what followed gave me a great laugh.

"Teacher," she began, "I think I understand now why you always say pronunciation and accent are more important than vocabulary and grammar!"

The previous weekend, Lian had traveled to Singapore for a short holiday. At the airport for her return flight, she approached the airline counter, intending to say, "Excuse me, I need to get my flight ticket. I have my passport ready."

What came out instead was: "Excuse me, I need to get my fried chicken. I have my passport ready."

The airline attendant looked confused. "You need... what?"

Thinking her English wasn't clear enough, Lian spoke louder and slower: "MY FRIED CHICKEN!"

By now, several travelers had turned to stare. The attendant, still puzzled, asked, "You want fried chicken? I'm sorry, but outside food isn't allowed through security."

Frustrated, Lian held up her passport and pointed at the departure board. "No! I need fried chicken to go there!"

A kind elderly gentleman in line behind her finally understood. "She needs her flight ticket," he explained to the attendant. "Not fried chicken." The attendant's face lit up with understanding, and everyone shared a good-natured laugh.

Lian got her boarding pass and made her way to the gate, but not before stopping at an actual fried chicken restaurant in the airport before boarding" just to make my words come true," she told me with a grin.

"So now," Lian concluded her story, "when I walked to the boarding gate, I really did have a passport and fried chicken in my hands!"

I laughed, but there was an important lesson beneath the humor. Lian's extensive vocabulary and good grammar couldn't help her when two mispronounced words completely changed her meaning.

After that day, Lian became a champion in pronunciation practice. She embraced the media immersion techniques from the Recall method, particularly watching airport and travel videos on YouTube. She would practice the troublesome "fl" sound by repeating "flight, flame, flower, floor" while watching herself in the mirror.

Six months later, when she traveled again, she proudly sent me a video message from the airport: "Hello teacher! I am at the airport and have my FLIGHT TICKET ready!" The distinction between those previously troublesome sounds was crystal clear. Lian's story reminds us that language isn't just about knowing words—it's about being understood. And sometimes, the difference between asking for your flight ticket and announcing you want fried chicken is just a matter of pronunciation and accent!

ACCENT ISSUES

Accents are a natural part of language. Everyone has an accent; our accent is part of our cultural identity.

A person's accent can significantly influence how well others understand them and impact their confidence while speaking. When your accent is very strong, listeners might struggle to follow you. They might ask you to repeat yourself often, making conversations frustrating for both sides.

Many English learners feel nervous or embarrassed about their accents. This concern can lead them to speak less or avoid certain situations. You shouldn't fall into this trap; there are solutions to address the accent issue.

THE SCIENCE OF ACCENTS

To understand accents, we must look at how our brains process language. When you learned your native language as a child, your brain formed specific neural pathways for certain sounds. By adulthood, these pathways are deeply established, and your brain automatically filters new languages.

When we speak, our words are shaped by how our mouths move, and each person's mouth moves differently based on their accent.

For example, if someone from the North of England says "book," their mouth might move quite differently from someone from the South of England saying the same word.

This can be tricky when talking to someone from a different part of the world with a different accent. They may be saying something like "bawk" instead of "book" to your ears. Even if you understand what they mean, it is hard to decipher their words, especially if they're speaking quickly or in stressful situations.

Your brain doesn't recognize that an accent is separate from language itself. The sounds, intonation, rhythm, and stress patterns are one package to your brain. This is why, when you speak English, your brain naturally applies the sound patterns of your native language.

For example, Spanish speakers often add an "e" sound before English words starting with "s" plus another consonant (saying "estation" instead of "station") because this sound combination doesn't exist in Spanish. Their brains are automatically applying Spanish pronunciation rules to English words. Yuki, a biologist from Japan, explained it perfectly: "When I speak English, my Japanese brain is like a pushy translator who keeps interrupting to say, 'No, no, that's not how we say it!'"

THE GOOD NEWS: YOUR ACCENT CAN CHANGE

It's often said that changing your accent after childhood is impossible. This is not true! Changing your accent requires conscious effort and consistent practice—it doesn't happen automatically when you know a language.

Remember how we discussed that your brain doesn't distinguish between language and accent? This works in your favor. When you expose yourself to large amounts of English spoken by native speakers, your brain gradually begins recognizing new sound patterns and learning to reproduce them.

Carlos, a Brazilian business executive, described his accent journey: "For years, I focused on vocabulary and grammar. My accent stayed Brazilian. Then, I started watching American TV shows for an hour daily and repeating phrases exactly as they sounded. After six months, my American clients started understanding me on the first try. After a year, some even asked if I had lived in the US!"

ACCENT NEUTRALIZATION VS. ACCENT ADOPTION

When dealing with accent issues, you have two practical approaches:

Path 1: Accent Neutralization

Accent neutralization doesn't mean erasing all traces of your native accent. Instead, it focuses on correcting the specific pronunciation patterns that cause misunderstandings.

Jeong-Min, a South Korean Engineering student, focused on the "f" and "p" sounds for three weeks, as Koreans don't have the "f" sound. "I practiced these sounds for 10 minutes daily," she told me. "I repeated words like 'fan, pan, fine, pine' until my mouth muscles learned the difference. English speakers understand me much better, even though I still have a Korean accent in other ways."

Benefits of Accent Neutralization

- Focuses on the most problematic sounds first.

- Yields faster results for basic understanding.

- Preserves some of your linguistic identity.

- It is usually easier than complete accent adoption.

Path 2: Accent Adoption

Adopting an accent requires extensive practice to speak like a native English speaker. This method involves training your ear to recognize and your mouth to reproduce a specific English accent's melody, rhythm, and unique sounds.

Ahmed, an Egyptian doctor working in London, adopted a British accent. "I chose one British actor whose voice I liked and watched his interviews repeatedly," he explained. "I recorded myself saying the same phrases and compared them.

After a year of this practice, my patients stopped asking me to repeat myself, and some even thought I had been educated in England!"

BENEFITS OF ACCENT ADOPTION:

- Can help you integrate more seamlessly in specific regions.

- Often leads to a better understanding by native speakers.

- May provide professional advantages in specific fields.

- Builds deeper awareness of the language.

CHAPTER 11

HOW MEDIA IMMERSION TRANSFORMS YOUR ACCENT

Here's something fascinating: many students who follow the media immersion methods we've discussed in earlier chapters report their accent improves even when they're not specifically working on it. This "passive improvement" happens because:

1. **Ear Training First**: By hearing correct pronunciation repeatedly, your brain begins recognizing proper sound patterns.

2. **Shadow Speaking Reprograms Muscle Memory**: When you repeat phrases exactly as you hear them, your mouth gradually learns new movements.

3. **Rhythm and Intonation Transfer Naturally**: Even before mastering individual sounds, the melody of English begins to influence your speech.

4. **Your Brain Makes Unconscious Corrections**: With enough exposure, your brain automatically adjusts toward the sounds it regularly hears.

Lina, a Spanish architect, experienced this unexpected benefit: "I was focusing on learning business vocabulary by watching design shows. After three months, my colleagues mentioned that my English sounded clearer. I hadn't even been working on my accent, but it improved anyway!"

YOUR MOUTH MUSCLE: EXERCISE IT
FOR BETTER PRONUNCIATION

One part of accent improvement that's often overlooked is the physical dimension. Speaking English may require using your lips, tongue, and throat in ways unfamiliar to speakers of other languages.

My student Pavel, a civil engineer from Poland, complained that the sounds of English hurt his mouth after a while. "My mouth would actually get tired after a workout," he said. This is normal! Your speaking muscles need training like any other muscle in your body.

Try these physical exercises to develop your English pronunciation muscles:

Tongue Twisters: Start slowly and gradually increase speed.

- "She sells seashells by the seashore."

- "Red lorry, yellow lorry."

- "Unique New York."

Exaggeration Exercises: Over-emphasize sounds that don't exist in your language.

- If you struggle with "th" sounds, practice sticking your tongue between your teeth and blowing air while saying"the, that, those, them."

- For the troublesome "r" sound, practice curling your tongue back slightly while saying "red, truck, around."

Mirror Work: Watch your mouth movements.

- Compare your mouth shape when saying problematic sounds to videos of native speakers.

- Record yourself on video to spot differences in lip and tongue positioning.

Ana, a Portuguese data scientist, made excellent progress by spending five minutes each morning making exaggerated mouth movements while saying challenging English sounds. "I felt silly, but it worked! After a month, these sounds started feeling natural instead of awkward."

HOW ACCENT AND CONFIDENCE AFFECT EACH OTHER

There's a fascinating relationship between accent and confidence that creates either a positive or negative cycle:

THE NEGATIVE CYCLE:

- You worry about your accent.

- This anxiety makes your pronunciation worse.

- Listeners struggle to understand you.

- Their reactions damage your confidence further.

- Lower confidence leads to even more pronunciation problems.

THE POSITIVE CYCLE:

- You focus on communicating. It need not be perfect.

- This relaxed attitude improves your pronunciation.

- Listeners understand you better.

- Their positive responses boost your confidence.

- Greater confidence leads to even more precise pronunciation.

Gabriela, a Venezuelan marketing professional, described breaking out of the negative cycle: "I used to panic whenever I had to speak English in meetings. My accent will get thicker when I am nervous, making everything worse. Then, I started practicing with podcasts daily until the sounds became automatic. Once I didn't have to think about each word, my confidence grew, and people stopped asking me to repeat myself."

COMMON ACCENT CHALLENGES BY LANGUAGE BACKGROUND

Different language backgrounds create distinct accent patterns in English. Here are common challenges and targeted exercises for various language groups:

For Spanish Speakers:

- Challenge: Adding an "e" before words starting with "s+consonant"

- Exercise: Practice words like "special, student, school" beginning directly with the "s" sound.

For Chinese Speakers:

- Challenge: Distinguishing between "l" and "r" sounds

- Exercise: Contrast pairs like "light/right, late/rate, long/wrong."

For Arabic Speakers:

- Challenge: The "p" sound (often pronounced as "b")

- Exercise: Practice minimal pairs like "pat/bat, pan/ban, cup/cub."

For French Speakers:

- Challenge: The "h" sound (often silent in French)

- Exercise: Practice emphasizing the "h" in words like "hello, house, behind."

For Japanese Speakers:

- Challenge: The "th" sounds (often pronounced as "s" or "z")

- Exercise: Practice phrases like "these three things" and "think about that."

Viktor, a Russian Police Officer, created his "English sound workout," focusing on the sounds that Russians typically struggle with. "I recorded native speakers saying words with 'w', 'th', and certain vowel sounds, then practiced repeating them for 10 minutes daily. It was like training for a sport – uncomfortable, but my mouth muscles eventually learned the new movements."

REAL-LIFE SUCCESS STORY:
STEFAN'S ACCENT TRANSFORMATION

Stefan, a German mechanical engineer, came to me with a common problem: despite excellent grammar and vocabulary, his heavy German accent made phone calls with English-speaking clients frustrating.

"Every call was the same," he told me. Sometimes, they will say, 'Excuse me?' I will repeat myself; they will understand or might ask me to spell it out. It was exhausting and embarrassing."

We Developed a Three-Part Plan:

1. Identify the most problematic sounds. We recorded Stefan speaking and found his three most significant pronunciation issues:

- The "w" sound (pronounced as "v")

- The "th" sound (pronounced as "z" or "s")

Sentence intonation (using German intonation instead of English patterns).

2. Create a focused daily practice routine. Stefan committed to:

- 10 minutes of targeted sound practice each morning.

- 20 minutes of shadow speaking with business podcasts during his commute.

- Watching one English TV episode each evening, pausing to repeat phrases.

3. Implement a "pronunciation first" approach. When learning new vocabulary, Stefan will master the pronunciation before focusing on using the word in sentences.

After three months, Stefan noticed that clients rarely asked him to repeat himself.

After six months, he managed complex phone negotiations with no pronunciation issues disrupting conversations.

"What surprised me most," Stefan said, "was that I didn't have to sound perfectly American. I had to fix the specific pronunciation problems that were causing misunderstandings. I still speak English with a slight German accent, but now it's charming rather than confusing!"

THINKING IN ENGLISH:
THE CONNECTION TO ACCENT IMPROVEMENT

There's a surprising relationship between thinking in English and improving your accent that many students overlook.

When you think in your native language and then translate to English, you're essentially processing language twice—first forming thoughts in your native sound system, then converting to English. This double processing often causes your native language's pronunciation patterns to carry over into your English speech.

Hiroshi, a business consultant from Japan, noticed this connection: "When I forced myself to think directly in English, I found my pronunciation improved. It's like my thoughts already had a Japanese accent, and when I translated them, that accent came through in my speech."

Developing the habit of thinking in English creates a more direct pathway from thoughts to speech, bypassing the interference from your native language's sound patterns.

This doesn't happen overnight, but you can encourage it by:

1. Narrating your daily activities to yourself in English.

2. Formulate your opinions on topics directly in English.

3. Dreaming in English: you can influence this by immersing yourself in English before sleep!

4. Counting and doing simple math in English.

Luisa, a Brazilian Pharmacist, placed sticky notes around her apartment with the prompt "Think in English" as reminders. "It felt artificial at first," she said, "but after a few weeks, I caught myself naturally thinking in English. My speaking became more fluid, and people commented that my pronunciation had improved."

YOUR ACCENT ACTION PLAN: PRACTICAL NEXT STEPS

Let's conclude with a practical plan you can start implementing today:

1. Assess Your Current Accent.

- Record yourself reading a paragraph in English.

- Ask a native speaker if the sounds are not clear.

- Identify 3-5 specific pronunciation issues to focus on first.

2. Create a Daily Practice Routine.

- 5 minutes: Targeted exercises for your specific problem sound.

- 10 minutes: Shadow speaking with explicit audio content.

- 15+ minutes: Immersive listening with content you enjoy.

3. Track Your Progress.

- Record the same paragraph every month.

- Note which sounds are improving and which need more work.

- Celebrate your progress—accent improvement takes time!

4. Incorporate Technology.

- Use pronunciation apps that provide feedback.

- Join online pronunciation groups for support.

- Try speech-to-text to test if your pronunciation is machine-recognizable.

Mei-Ling, a software developer from China, said it best: "Changing your accent is like learning a dance – awkward at first, but eventually, your body remembers the movements without you having to think about each step."

Your accent journey is personal and unique. Some sounds will come quickly; others may require persistent practice.

CHAPTER 12

MASTERING ENGLISH THROUGH ONLINE QUIZZES

Vocabulary • Grammar • Phrasal Verbs • Idioms

In earlier chapters, we explored various parts of English language learning, from listening and speaking to reading and writing. In this chapter, we'll discuss the effectiveness of online quizzes in mastering these areas and how repetition is the key to learning.

Why Online Quizzes Work So Well

Online quizzes help you learn English better and faster. They make improving your vocabulary, grammar, phrasal verbs, and idioms easy. Here's why they work so well:

1. **Easy to Access:** You can take online quizzes wherever you are — at home, on the bus, or during lunch breaks. This makes learning fit into your busy life.

2. **Made Just for You:** These quizzes can be adjusted to match your learning needs. If you struggle with grammar but excel at vocabulary, you can focus more on grammar practice.

3. **Learn from Mistakes Right Away:** After finishing a quiz, you immediately see what you got right and wrong. This helps you understand your strengths and weaknesses without waiting.

Online quizzes turn learning English into something you can do anytime, anywhere, and in a way that works best for you.

REPETITION: THE KEY TO LEARNING

The Power of Repetition in Language Learning

Repetition is key to mastering a new language. When you revisit the same material multiple times, you build stronger skills and remember more. Here's how to use repetition effectively:

1. **Spaced Repetition Systems (SRS)**

   - What it is: Use apps like Anki or Quizlet (found on the internet) to review flashcards continuously.

   - Why it works: Information is reviewed just before you forget it, strengthening memory.

2. **Role-Playing Practice**

   - What it is: Practice real-life conversations repeatedly (ordering food, making appointments).

   - Why it works: Builds confidence for actual situations you'll encounter.

3. **Shadowing Native Speakers**

   - What it is: Listen to native speakers and repeat exactly what they say, matching their tone.

   - Why it works: Improves your pronunciation and speaking rhythm.

4. **Storytelling Practice**

   - What it is: Retell stories multiple times, focusing on different aspects each time.

- Why it works: It helps you use language creatively while reinforcing your learning.

5. **Language Games**

- What it is: Play word games that require repeatedly using the same language elements.

- Why it works: It makes repetition fun and keeps you motivated.

6. **Daily Practice Routines**

- What it is: Set up regular habits like daily journaling or speaking practice.

- Why it works: Consistency is important for long-term language learning.

7. **Group Repetition**

- What it is: Practice phrases with other learners.

- Why it works: Reduces anxiety and builds confidence.

8. **Recording Yourself**

- What it is: Record your speaking, listen back, and practice improvements.

- Why it works: Helps you hear and fix your own mistakes.

9. **Using Words in Different Contexts**

- What it is: Practice the same vocabulary in various situations and activities.

- Why it works: Shows how language works flexibly in real-life.

Taking Online Quizzes Successfully

- Target: Aim for a 70% or higher score on each quiz.

- Repeat quiz: Take quizzes multiple times until you reach your target.

Common Quiz Mistakes to Avoid

1. Read instructions carefully before starting.
2. Take your time - rushing leads to careless errors.
3. Always review your answers before submitting.

CONCLUSION

Online quizzes offer a range of benefits, including convenience, flexibility, immediate feedback, and repetition. Repeating questions and exercises can build confidence, improve accuracy, and develop fluency.

EXERCISE

Take an online quiz to test your knowledge, choose one that focuses on areas you need improvement in, and take your time answering questions. Repeat the process several times until you score 70% or more.

CHAPTER 13

MASTERING SILENT LETTERS IN ENGLISH VOCABULARY

Let's now focus on an essential part of English vocabulary: silent letters. Silent letters can be a significant challenge for learners, as they can make it difficult to pronounce words correctly. This chapter will discuss the best solution for pronouncing words with one or more silent letters.

EXAMPLES OF SILENT LETTERS

Here are examples of words with silent letters:

1. **Knight**: The "k" is silent, and the word is pronounced as "night".

2. **Psychology**: The "p" is silent, and the word is pronounced as "sai-kol-uh-jee".

3. **Island**: The "s" is silent, and the word is pronounced as "ai-luhnd".

4. **Gnome**: The "g" is silent, and the word is pronounced as "nohm".

5. **Wrist**: The "w" is silent, and the word is pronounced as "rist".

HOW TO LEARN WORDS WITH SILENT LETTERS

Here are tips for learning words with silent letters:

1. **Listen to Native Speakers**: pay attention to how native speakers pronounce words that have silent letters; this is an

excellent method to improve your pronunciation skills!

2. **Practice, Practice, Practice**: Make it a habit to pronounce words with silent letters regularly. This small practice can significantly enhance your muscle memory and improve your pronunciation!

3. **Focus on Word Families**: words that end in "-ight" or "-ite". This will help you learn patterns and improve your pronunciation.

4. **Read Aloud**: When reading aloud, focus on words that have silent letters. This practice will enhance your pronunciation abilities and boost your fluency.

COMMON SILENT LETTER PATTERNS

Here are some common silent letter patterns to look out for:

1. **-ight**: The "g" is often silent in words that end in "-ight", such as "night", "light", and "sight".

2. **-ite**: The "i" is often silent in words that end in "-ite", such as "site", "cite", and "excite".

3. **-gn**: The "g" is often silent in words that start with "gn", such as "gnat", "gnome", and "gnostic".

4. **-kn**: The "k" is often silent in words that start with "kn", such as "knight", "knob", and "knock".

5. **-ps**: The "p" is often silent in words that start with "ps", such as "psychology", "psychiatry", and "psychic".

Here are the top twenty most commonly spoken words in the English language with silent letters:

1. **Knight** (silent "k")

2. **Psychology** (silent "p")

3. **Island** (silent "s")

4. **Gnome** (silent "g")

5. **Wrist** (silent "w")

6. **Wrong** (silent "w")

7. **Write** (silent "w")

8. **Rhythm** (silent "h")

9. **Ghost** (silent "h")

10. **Hour** (silent "h")

11. **Heir** (silent "h")

12. **Honest** (silent "h")

13. **Knead** (silent "k")

14. **Knob** (silent "k")

15. **Knot** (silent "k")

16. **Night** (silent "gh")

17. **Light** (silent "gh")

18. **Right** (silent "gh")

19. **Sight** (silent "gh")

20. **Thought** (silent "gh")

Note that the frequency of these words can vary depending on the context. However, these twenty words are considered among the most common words with silent letters in English.

Here are more notes on the silent letters in these words:

1. The "k" in **knight, knead, knob,** and **knot** is silent because it comes before the letter "n".

2. The "p" in **psychology** is silent because it comes before the letter "s".

3. The "s" in **island** is silent because it comes before the letter "l".

4. The "g" in **gnome** is silent as it comes before the letter "n".

5. The "w" in **wrist, wrong,** and **write** is silent because it comes before the letter "r".

6. The "h" in **rhythm, ghost, hour, heir, honest,** and **thought** is silent because it comes at the beginning of the word or before a vowel.

7. The "gh" in **night**, **light**, **right**, **sight**, and **thought** is silent because it comes in the middle or at the end of the word.

CONCLUSION

Silent letters can be a significant challenge for learners, but with practice and patience, it is possible to master them. Learning each word individually and focusing on word families can improve their pronunciation and develop a more natural-sounding accent. Remember to listen to native speakers, practice regularly, and use online resources to learn the correct pronunciation of words with silent letters.

EXERCISE

Choose a word with a silent letter, such as "knight" or "psychology". Practice pronouncing the word regularly and focus on developing a natural-sounding accent. Use online resources, such as pronunciation guides and videos, to learn the correct pronunciation.

Read aloud regularly and pay attention to words with silent letters. With consistent practice and patience, you can master silent letters and improve your English pronunciation.

CHAPTER 14

THE RECALL TOTAL ENGLISH METHOD –
PUTTING IT ALL TOGETHER

As we near the end of our journey, let's review what we've learned and see how everything fits together. The Recall Total English method stands on five essential pillars—the foundation of the entire program. By understanding these five core pillars, you'll understand the complete program and be able to implement it more effectively.

PILLAR 1: MEANINGFUL EXPOSURE AND
ACTIVE PRODUCTION RECOGNITION

Meaningful exposure means being around English content that is important to you.

This method uses a basic idea about how our brains learn: we focus more on information that interests, excites, or helps us.

When you encounter words in situations that matter to you, your brain sends out chemicals like dopamine that help you remember things better. These brain chemicals mark the information as "important," making it easier to remember later.

This explains why you might easily remember dialogue from a favorite movie but struggle to recall vocabulary from a textbook.

Hiroshi, a Japanese engineering student, experienced this firsthand. He had studied English for years with limited progress. Then, he discovered a YouTube channel about motorcycle repair—his passion. After three months of watching videos he enjoyed, his technical English vocabulary improved significantly, even though he never planned to study what he was learning. "The difference," Hiroshi explained, "was that I actually cared about understanding every detail of what was being said. I replayed parts I didn't fully understand, not because I was forcing myself to study, but because I wanted to know how to adjust that carburetor!"

The Hiroshi example demonstrates that you are more likely to learn effectively if you expose yourself to meaningful content that interests you. This builds strong "recognition pathways" in your brain—meaning you can understand the language. However, as Hiroshi later discovered, this was not enough without production practice (speaking and writing). Hiroshi had achieved only one-half of two parts in mastering his English skills.

PRODUCTION

Take Andrei, a professional cook from Romania, as an example. He, like Hiroshi, spent many hours enjoying content that was enjoyable to him. Andrei loved watching English movies; over the years, he had seen dozens of them with subtitles. Because of this, he got good at understanding English. He could follow conversations, catch jokes, and even notice subtle meanings in the dialogue.

But when it came to speaking English himself, he found it much harder. He often struggled to find the right words, form sentences, or express his thoughts clearly.

This happened because Andrei had primarily focused on passive learning (recognition), listening, and reading—without practicing active skills like (production) speaking and writing. Watching movies helped him understand English but didn't help him produce the language himself effectively. This is a common challenge for many language learners. They can understand a lot because their brain has learned to recognize the language, but they can't speak well because they haven't trained their brain to create the language independently. What is important to understand here is that recognition and production are important; to become fluent, you must balance both.

PRACTICAL IMPLEMENTATION

Follow Your Genuine Interests: Be honest about what engages you, not what you think should interest you. Love cooking? Watch cooking shows. Are you fascinated by astronomy? Find podcasts about space. Enjoy romantic comedies? Watch as many as you can.

Diversify Your Content Types: Even within your interests, use various media formats to engage different learning pathways in your brain:

- Visual learners will benefit more from videos and games.

- Auditory learners will absorb more from podcasts and audiobooks.

- Reading-oriented learners will connect with articles and books.

Create an Immersion Environment: Surround yourself with English throughout your day:

- Set your phone and social media accounts to English.

- Follow English-speaking accounts related to your hobbies.

- Join online communities where English is the common language.

- Label household items with English terms (yes, this old technique works!)

Layer Your Exposure: To build confidence, start with the content you can mostly understand (about 70% understanding), then gradually introduce more challenging material.

During class, I often ask students to rate how much they genuinely enjoy their current English learning materials on a scale of 1-10. People who score below seven always struggle with consistency and retention. Your brain won't focus on information if it considers it uninteresting or unimportant.

María, a Spanish marketing executive, transformed her English when she stopped forcing herself through business English textbooks (which she rated a "4" for enjoyment) and instead immersed herself in marketing podcasts by hosts whose style she loved (rated "9"). "I went from dreading my English practice to looking forward to it," she said. "And suddenly words and phrases I'd been struggling to memorize started coming naturally in conversation."

PILLAR 2: ACTIVE ENGAGEMENT

The science behind it

While meaningful exposure creates the foundation, active

engagement builds the structure of your English fluency. Your brain learns more effectively when interacting with information rather than passively consuming it.

Neurologically, passive exposure primarily activates recognition pathways in your brain. You might recognize words and phrases when you hear them, but these pathways aren't strongly connected to your speech production systems.

Active engagement creates and strengthens the neural connections between recognition and production, enabling you to understand and use the language.

PRACTICAL IMPLEMENTATION

To incorporate active engagement in your learning:

Shadow Speaking: This powerful technique involves repeating what you hear right after the speaker, matching their pronunciation, rhythm, and intonation as closely as possible. It creates muscle memory for English speech patterns and helps your brain connect hearing with speaking.

Start with short phrases, then gradually work up to longer sentences. Fatima, a souvenir store owner from Morocco, practiced shadow speaking with TED talks for 10 minutes daily. "After two months, I noticed English sentences forming in my mind more naturally, as if my brain had absorbed the rhythms of the language."

Talk Back to Your Media: Pause videos or podcasts, respond to what you've heard:

- Answer questions posed by hosts or characters.

- Give your opinion on the topics discussed.

- Predict what might happen next.

- Summarize what you've understood so far.

Peter, a data analyst from Germany, made this a game while watching TV shows. "Whenever a character asks a question, I pause and answer as if they were talking to me. It made watching shows both entertaining and productive."

Create Content, Not Just Consume It: Producing English content accelerates your progress dramatically:

- Record voice notes summarizing articles you've read.

- Leave comments on English YouTube videos or social media posts.

- Join discussions in forums about topics that interest you.

- Keep a simple audio or written journal in English.

The production effort forces your brain to solidify pathways between your thoughts and English expression.

Body-Mind Connection: Involve your body in learning with these techniques:

- Use gestures while speaking to anchor phrases in muscle memory.

- Read aloud while walking to associate language with movement.

- Act out scenarios with full expressions and movements.

- Draw simple pictures to represent new phrases or ideas.

Sofia, a Brazilian Law student, created physical gestures for challenging grammar ideas like perfect tenses. "When I use the gesture while speaking, the correct form comes more naturally. It's like my hands remember even when my brain gets confused."

The 50/50 Rule: For ideal learning, speak or write for at least half the time you spend listening or reading. This balance ensures you're building both recognition and production skills.

PILLAR 3: CONFIDENCE BUILDING

The Science Behind It

As I explained in an earlier chapter, confidence affects your ability to use English. This isn't psychological—it's neurobiological. Anxiety triggers your brain's stress response, redirecting resources from your prefrontal cortex (responsible for language processing) to more primitive brain regions concerned with survival.

Simply put, when you're nervous about speaking English, your brain has less language processing power. This creates the common experience where you "know" the words but can't access them during stressful speaking situations.

The confidence building pillar works by gradually training your brain to associate English use with positive experiences rather than stress and judgment.

This rewires your neural responses, keeping your prefrontal cortex engaged even in challenging situations. Mei, a Chinese business student, described this transformation vividly:

"Before, speaking English in meetings felt like solving complex math while performing on stage – my mind would freeze. After building confidence through the recall method, it began feeling more like conversing with friends. The knowledge was the same, but my ability to access it completely changed."

PRACTICAL IMPLEMENTATION

To build unshakable confidence in your English abilities:

Create a Safety Zone: Arrange English-speaking experiences from least to challenging and systematically work your way up:

1. Speaking English alone (recording yourself).
2. Speaking with one supportive friend.
3. Small group conversations with patient listeners.
4. Larger group settings.
5. Professional contexts or public speaking.

Celebrate Small Victories: Train your brain to notice success instead of fixating on mistakes:

- Keep a "victory journal" recording moments of successful communication.

- Acknowledge when native speakers understand you without asking for clarification.

- Recognize when you express complex thoughts without reverting to your native language.

- Celebrate understanding challenging content that would have been impossible months earlier.

These positive rewards lead to a cycle where having confidence encourages more practice, which boosts confidence even more.

Ahmed, a doctor from Egypt, came up with what he called "conversation anchors"—simple phrases he could use to organize his thoughts before giving more detailed explanations. "These reliable phrases keep me from freezing up. They're like steppingstones that help me cross the river of conversation."

Visualize Successful Communication: Mental rehearsal activates many of the same neural pathways as actual practice:

- Before meaningful conversations, spend 5 minutes imagining the interaction going smoothly.

- Picture yourself speaking confidently and others responding positively.

- Mentally rehearse, managing potential challenges calmly.

Yuko, a Japanese marketing professional, used visualization before client calls. "I imagine the entire conversation flowing naturally, with me understanding everything and responding clearly. When the actual call happens, my brain already has a successful template to follow."

Reframe Language Goals: Shift focus from perfect accuracy to successful communication:

- Judge interactions by whether you conveyed your meaning, not whether you made zero mistakes.

- Remember that even native speakers make grammar errors in casual conversation.

- Value making yourself understood over sounding like a perfect English speaker.

PILLAR 4: CONSISTENT PRACTICE

The Science Behind It

Consistency powerfully affects language learning because our brains form and strengthen neural connections. You maintain and strengthen these pathways when you practice regularly, even for short periods.

But if there are long breaks between practice sessions, the connections weaken, making it harder to strengthen them again. Research in neuroscience shows that practicing regularly in shorter sessions helps people remember things better over the long-term than cramming all the studying into a few intense sessions.

This explains why studying English for 20 minutes daily typically gets better results than a single 2-hour session once a week.

Consistent practice relies on habit formation. When practicing English becomes as automatic as brushing your teeth, you save mental energy deciding when and how to engage in practice.

Carlo, an Italian software developer, tracked his progress over six months. "I compared two approaches: studying three hours every Sunday versus 30 minutes every day. The difference was remarkable. With daily practice, I retained vocabulary better, felt more confident speaking, and enjoyed the process more."

PRACTICAL IMPLEMENTATION

To build consistency into your English development:

Establish Minimum Viable Practice: Set a non-negotiable daily minimum so low it feels almost impossible to skip:

- 5 minutes of shadow speaking

- Listening to one short podcast episode

- Reading one page of English content

- Writing three sentences in a journal

On days when you have energy and time, you'll naturally do more, but this minimum ensures you never break the chain of practice. Consistency itself matters more than quantity.

Habit Stacking: Attach English practice to existing habits to make it automatic:

- Listen to English podcasts while commuting.

- Watch English YouTube videos while exercising.

- Read English news while having morning coffee.

- Listen to audiobooks while doing household chores.

My student Raj, a busy doctor from India, "habit-stacked" his English practice by listening to medical podcasts while walking his dog each morning. "I never have to decide when to practice English – it's part of my dog-walking routine now. Both my English and my dog get their daily exercise!"

Consistency Tracking: Use simple systems to track your practice streak:

- Mark completed days on a calendar.

- Use habit-tracking apps.

- Create a visual progress bar for your monthly goal.

Seeing your unbroken streak motivates you, making you reluctant to break the chain.

Recovery Protocol: Plan how you'll get back on track when you inevitably miss a day:

- Never miss two days in a row.

- If you miss a day, start again with the minimum practice.

- Don't try to "make up" for missed days—this creates an overwhelming backlog.

- Focus on reestablishing the habit, not punishing yourself for the lapse.

PILLAR 5: PERSONAL CONNECTION

Express Your Authentic Self: Practice expressing your genuine thoughts and experiences:

- Write a journal about your feelings and experiences, not generic topics.

- Share personal stories (even if only recorded for yourself).

- Express opinions about topics you genuinely care about.

- Find words for your values, dreams, and beliefs in English.

Build Relationships Through English: Create connections where English is the medium:

- Find language exchange partners with shared interests.

- Join international communities focused on your hobbies.

- Take part in English discussion groups (in-person or online).

- Build professional relationships with English-speaking colleagues.

The emotional reward of connection provides powerful motivation for improvement.

Cultural Exploration: Connect with cultures through authentic English content:

- Follow customs and celebrations from English-speaking regions.

- Try recipes while watching English cooking demonstrations.

- Learn about history and traditions through documentaries.

- Explore music, art, and literature that you find interesting.

Ana, a Spanish art student, deepened her connection to English by exploring American abstract expressionism. "Learning about Jackson Pollock and Mark Rothko in English helped me associate the language with something I'm passionate about. Now, English feels like a part of my identity as someone who loves art."

Digital Identity Development: Create parts of your online presence in English:

- Maintain social media accounts in English.

- Join discussions in English language forums.

- Create content (blog posts, videos, comments) in English.

- Build a professional profile on international platforms.

These activities help you develop a version of yourself comfortably in English.

Languages of the Heart: Connect English to your emotional world:

- Find songs that move you and learn to sing along.

- Watch movies that make you laugh or cry.

- Express affection or encouragement to others in English.

- Find quotes or poems that move feelings in you.

CHAPTER 15

PUTTING THE FIVE PILLARS TOGETHER: DAILY PRACTICE

Let's see how these five pillars work together in your daily practice. Here's what a typical day will look like when applying the complete Recall Total English method:

MORNING ROUTINE (15-20 minutes):

- Listen to an English podcast about a topic you love while getting ready (Meaningful Exposure).

- Repeat interesting phrases aloud as you hear them (Active Engagement).

- Note one new expression you want to use later (Personal Connection).

- Track your morning practice in a habit app (Consistent Practice).

Celebrate understanding something challenging (Confidence Building).

COMMUTE OR LUNCH BREAK (10-15 MINUTES):

- Use a language app or watch a short YouTube video (Consistent Practice).

- Respond aloud to what you've watched or heard (Active Engagement).

- Connect content to your own experiences or opinions (Personal Connection).

- Try understanding without subtitles as a gentle challenge (Confidence Building).

- Choose content that genuinely interests you (Meaningful Exposure).

EVENING ROUTINE (20-30 MINUTES):

- Watch part of an English TV episode or play a game in English (Meaningful Exposure).

- Talk back to the characters or summarize what happened (Active Engagement).

- Share something interesting you learned with a friend or in an online community (Personal Connection).

- Notice how much more you understand than when you started (Confidence Building).

- Maintain your daily streak, even if you're tired (Consistent Practice).

BEFORE BED (OPTIONAL BUT POWERFUL):

- Listen to English audio at a low volume as you fall asleep (Supporting your brain's night shift).

- Choose calm, clearly spoken content you've already heard while awake.

- Set a timer so it doesn't play all night.

- Notice if certain words or phrases come more easily the next day.

WEEKLY SPECIAL ACTIVITIES:

- Weekend movie night in English (Meaningful Exposure + Consistent Practice)

- Online language exchange conversation (Confidence Building + Personal Connection)

- Game night with international players (Active Engagement + Meaningful Exposure)

- Weekly progress review and plan change (Supporting all pillars)

This integrated approach creates a virtuous cycle where each pillar reinforces the others. Regular practice builds confidence, which helps you connect with others, leading to more important experiences and greater involvement. The positive cycle continues.

REAL-LIFE SUCCESS CASE: ELENA'S TRANSFORMATION

Let me share how one of my students, Elena, an accountant from Ukraine, used the Recall method to transform her English in just six months. She had studied English for years but still struggled with speaking confidently. She knew lots of vocabulary and grammar but froze during conversations.

ELENA'S STARTING POINT:

- Could read English marketing materials without problems.

- Understood movies with subtitles.

- Became nervous when speaking and couldn't find words.

- Avoided international calls at work.

ELENA'S TRANSFORMATION

After implementing the Recall Total English method, Elena's progress was remarkable:

Within the first month, she established a daily routine of listening to marketing podcasts during her commute and watching one episode of her favorite show each evening.

By month three, she participated in international marketing webinars, asking questions without pre-writing them.

After six months, she volunteered to lead an English language presentation to international clients—something she would have declined before.

Elena reported that English no longer felt like a foreign language she had to translate in her head. "Now it feels like another way to be myself," she explained.

"I don't think about speaking English anymore—I just think about what I want to say."

THE PATH FORWARD

Learning English need not be a chore. Following the Recall Total English method becomes one of the most enjoyable parts of your day.

Imagine:

1. Watching your favorite shows and improving your English while being entertained.

2. Playing video games that connect you with people around the world.

3. Discovering podcasts that feed your curiosity while strengthening your listening skills.

4. Expressing your authentic self in a language spoken by nearly two billion people worldwide.

The beauty of this method is that it transforms "study time" into "enjoyment time." As my student Marco, a café waiter from Italy said: "For the first time in my life, I'm not studying English—I'm living it."

THE JOY OF FLUENCY

A special kind of joy comes with expressing yourself fluently in another language. It's like discovering a new room in a house you've lived in for years—suddenly, you have more space to be yourself, more ways to connect with others, and more windows to view the world.

My student Adina, an art student from Hungary, described this feeling beautifully: "When I started thinking and dreaming in English, it wasn't like I became a different person. It was like I became more of myself—like I found colors I didn't know I could paint with."

This joy is waiting for you. Not after years of grueling study, but starting today, as you begin applying the principles in this book.

CONSISTENCY IS KEY

The more you practice, the easier it becomes to recall words and form sentences. Aim to spend at least 60 minutes daily on English language-related activities, such as reading, writing, or speaking with a language human partner or AI partner.

Supplement your learning with language learning apps that offer daily challenges and games to keep things fun and interesting. Surround yourself with the language as much as possible.

Watch English movies and TV shows and listen to podcasts and audiobooks to expose yourself to naturally-spoken English. Read English books and articles and immerse yourself in English-speaking communities online. The more you expose yourself to the language, the more familiar it will become and the easier it will be to understand and communicate. Don't forget about vocabulary building. The more words you know, the better you can communicate your thoughts and ideas.

Make a habit of reading and writing down new words you encounter and use tools like flashcards or online quizzes to evaluate your knowledge regularly.

Actively seeking out synonyms and antonyms can help you remember words more effectively. Push yourself out of your comfort zone. Try writing or speaking about unfamiliar topics or challenging your current skill level. This will help you expand your vocabulary and improve your grammar. As you progress, don't be afraid to seek feedback on your language skills. Ask a native speaker, a teacher, or an AI to review your writing or speaking to find ways to improve. Their insights can help you refine your skills further and speed up your progress.

I want you to remember something important: the English you need is already inside you. Through years of exposure to movies, music, internet content, and perhaps formal study, your brain has collected thousands of English words, phrases, and expressions.

The Recall Total English method isn't about stuffing more information into your brain—it's about activating what's already there. It's about building bridges between your passive and active knowledge. It's about transforming English from something you study to something you live.

TUTORING INFORMATION

YOUR JOURNEY DOESN'T END HERE!

To further develop your English-speaking abilities, here are some resources that can complement your learning journey:

Online English Tutor Services ★★★★★

- **Italki**: Connect with certified English teachers worldwide for personalized one-on-one video lessons. Choose instructors based on their teaching style, rates, and availability. Many tutors offer conversation practice sessions specifically designed to improve your speaking confidence.

- **Preply**: Find tutors who specialize in conversation skills, business English, or exam preparation. Schedule regular sessions to practice speaking in a supportive environment where you'll receive immediate feedback on pronunciation and grammar.

- **Cambly:** Connect with native English speakers anytime, 24/7 via video calls. The platform offers flexible scheduling, allowing for quick 15-minute conversations or longer sessions of up to an hour. You can choose between group classes or private one-on-one sessions.

Language Learning Apps

Language Learning Apps ★ ★ ★ ★ ★

- **Duolingo**: Improve your speaking through fun, game-like exercises that prompt you to repeat phrases and sentences. The app uses speech recognition technology to help refine your pronunciation.

- **Babbel**: Focus on practical conversation skills with lessons designed by language experts. The app includes speech recognition to evaluate your pronunciation and provides dialogues based on real-life situations.

- **Rosetta Stone**: Immerse yourself in English through their TruAccent® speech recognition technology, which helps you fine-tune your accent. Practice speaking in various scenarios through their interactive activities.

A Personal Note to the Reader

Remember that language learning is a personal journey of growth and connection. Some ideas in this book will click right away, while others might take time or not click at all. This is part of the natural learning process. What matters most is that you enjoy the journey. When you find pleasure in the process, consistency follows naturally. When consistency becomes a habit, progress becomes inevitable—and then fluency.

Regular practice will keep your fluency active and ready to use. Without practice, the fluency you achieve can slip into long-term memory and become passive knowledge, where it's harder to access when you need it.

I wish you a life filled with new opportunities and the confidence to use your improved English skills whenever and wherever you need them. May your future be prosperous and your connections deep.

Book Website

VISIT THIS BOOK'S WEBSITE FOR MORE LEARNING RESOURCES

The website is regularly updated with new content based on the latest resources available for English language learners of all levels.

https://ddvujic.com/recall-total-english

About the Author

D. D. VUJIC is an international film producer, screenwriter, and best-selling author. Creative writing professor and English teacher. He is also a popular writer for hire and story and production consultant. His works include various international feature films, TV films, and TV series, as well as novels, short stories, and articles for producers and publishers in Europe, North America, and Asia. He has ghostwritten many personal memoirs, books, and screenplays, published in several languages, and is a favorite guest speaker among many international literary clubs.

Visit: D. D. Vujic

Official website: https://ddvujic.com/

Email: d.dan.vujic@gmail.com

Facebook: https://www.facebook.com/dan.vujic.3/

Instagram: https://www.instagram.com/d.danielvujic/

New book by D. D. Vujic for 2025

The true story behind the making of the movie *6 Days Dark*, whom many believe is cursed.

During the production, a third of the eighty-six cast and crew members that were married or in a relationship cheated on their partners. By the time *6 Days Dark* was released, most of them had divorced or separated.

Nine cast and crew members committed suicide, had fatal accidents, or died from illnesses and other causes. Several were jailed, one for multiple murders.

Many suffered from sudden unusual weight gain from which they struggled to get under control. Most had a significant pause in their careers, while others saw an end to their careers.

The movie itself is a thriller about adultery, murder and an ancient gypsy curse that drives people mad.

The story is written by the movie's writer-producer.

Visit the *6 DAYS DARK: Now Playing* official book website at **www.ddvujic.com/6-days-dark**

New book by D. D. Vujic for 2024

Nikola Tesla is credited for inventing the foundation of today's electronics and appliances, including electric cars, wireless communication, smartphones and the Internet. History portrays him as an eccentric recluse who abstained from alcohol, cigarettes, and lived a celibate life; but his personal secrets have remained hidden until now.

A recent discovery in the basement of the official Tesla Museum in Belgrade, Serbia, reveals hidden artifacts that challenge this carefully constructed narrative, including passionate love letters disclosing a secret romance, proof of his surprising friendship with notorious Mafia boss Charles 'Lucky' Luciano, and incomplete drawings and partial schematics for a radio that can communicate with the past.

These artifacts paint a different picture of Tesla, and the book raises the question is our present the one that was meant to be or was it altered. Written by bestselling biographer Sharon Rich and Tesla historian and bestselling author, screenwriter D. D. Vujic.

Visit the official *Tesla: Manhattan Dove to Queens Seagull* website at: **www.teslanovel.com**